Destined to Live
A True Story of a
Child in the Holocaust

Other books you might be interested in:

Survivors: True Stories of Children in the Holocaust
by Allan Zullo and Mara Bovsun

Heroes of the Holocaust
by Allan Zullo and Mara Bovsun

Destined to Live
A True Story of a
Child in the Holocaust

by Ruth Gruener
with Rachel Klein

Scholastic Inc.
New York   Toronto   London   Auckland   Sydney
Mexico City   New Delhi   Hong Kong   Buenos Aires

To my always supportive husband and family.
And, most of all, to the memory of all those who did not
survive to tell their stories.

Thank you to Mara Bovsun for
encouraging me to write.

ISBN-13: 978-0-439-89204-9
ISBN-10: 0-439-89204-X

12 11 10 9 8 7 6 5 4 3   8 9 10 11 12/0

Printed in the U.S.A.   40
First printing, October 2007

Introduction: The Holocaust

The Holocaust took place during World War II, when Adolf Hitler led his Nazi army in an attempt to eradicate all the Jews in Europe. The Nazis invaded Poland in the fall of 1939. At the beginning of that year, there were about seven million Jewish people living in Central and Eastern Europe. By war's end, approximately six million of them had been killed. About three million of those murdered were of Polish origin. Roughly 222,000 other people were persecuted as well, including Gypsies, homosexuals, Jehovah's Witnesses, and the physically disabled.

The Holocaust didn't happen overnight. A few years

before the war began, Jewish people were being ostracized, especially in Germany. They were turned away from social functions and their businesses suffered.

Then, on November 9, 1938, the situation in Germany worsened. For two nights, more than 8,000 Jewish homes, businesses, and synagogues were ransacked. Instigated by Nazi party officials, non-Jewish citizens took to the streets, smashing the glass windows of Jewish-owned stores. This became known as *Kristallnacht,* or the Night of Broken Glass.

As tensions worsened, Jewish people were beaten and shot in public places, and many were taken to camps where they were incarcerated, used as slave labor, or killed. They were called labor camps, concentration camps, or death camps. Conditions at these camps were awful, and many Jewish people perished in them. Auschwitz, in Poland, was the largest camp. Among the countless other concentration camps were Bergen-Belsen, Treblinka, and Dachau.

Many Jews who escaped the reach of the Nazis went into hiding. Some were taken in by Gentiles—non-Jews, usually Christians—who risked their own lives to save the lives of others.

When the war ended in 1945, those still alive in the camps were liberated, and people came out of hiding. They were the survivors of one of the worst atrocities humankind has ever seen — and hopefully ever will.

Prologue

How lovely my walks home from school have been lately, with spring arriving and the trees and flowers beginning to bloom in Brooklyn's Prospect Park! The air is so clean and fresh and the sun so bright, it's hard for me not to raise my face to the sky like a sunflower, basking in the warmth and the balmy breeze. Sometimes I stop and sit on one of the benches to watch children play on the green or to admire well-dressed young men and women strolling.

And then there are the small things that go on around me that you only notice if you look very carefully, like a line of ants marching along the crack of a sidewalk with crumbs of bread, or a mother bending down to wipe the remnants of a sticky red lollipop off her son's mouth, or two people passing and exchanging a smile. It's all so wonderful. I don't think that there will ever come a day when I take the simple things of this world for granted. Almost losing one's life, as I nearly did not too long ago, changes a person.

I am a teenager, living in Brooklyn, New York, in the United States of America. But I have traveled a long way to arrive here, and experienced so much. Some might say I was lucky. Others might say I was destined to live.

Part I: The Beginning

I was born in the early 1930s, on a warm Monday evening in August. My mother, Barbara Gamzer, a pretty woman with black hair and light blue eyes, delivered me at home, in a house on Wolynska Street, in the city of Lvov, in Poland.

I was given the Hebrew name Rachel Tcharne to honor the memories of my late grandmother and great-aunt. My Polish name on my birth certificate was Aurelia Czeslava. At first, I was called Rela, then Relunia, which was shortened to Lunia, or to my favorite nickname, Luncia.

I lived with my mother and my father, Isaac Gamzer — whom I called Tatu (Polish for Daddy) — in a large, two-bedroom apartment. Before the war began, my life was enviably sweet — quite literally. My parents owned a candy shop called Sarotina, and I would sneak treats whenever I could — pastries filled with rich cream, chocolate-covered jelly rings, little cakes with colorful icing. But my favorite was ice cream, which wasn't as sneakable. One year, we got an amazing ice-cream machine that had all different colors on a wheel that turned around. When my parents placed it in the window, our store became even more popular.

We did very well with the store and had many loyal customers, so I never wanted for anything. I had a beautiful bedroom with a canopy bed, and on my shelves were rows of handmade dolls and board games like checkers and chess. My closet was filled with the most gorgeous dresses, made of the finest cotton for summer and wool and velvet for winter. Wherever I went, people would say that I looked just like a doll, so perfectly coordinated and neat, with hats to match my dresses and black-and-white patent leather shoes on my feet. Before I started going to school, I had a nanny who would take me to the park every day to play. Before we returned home I was always allowed to stop at Sarotina and choose anything I wanted out of the case for after dinner.

I loved nothing better than holidays. Since we were Jewish, we had our own special holidays, such as Rosh Hashana, Yom Kippur, Hanukkah, Passover, and Purim. Purim was my favorite. Purim is a joyous Jewish festival. It honors the delivery of the Jews of Persia (now Iran) from an evil plot to destroy them. The name Purim comes from the Persian word *pur*, which means lot. Lots had been drawn to fix a day for the massacre of the Jews. Purim occurs in the spring, and children dress up in costumes and enjoy treats such as *hamantaschen*, a cookie filled with poppy seeds or chocolate.

But my parents made sure I didn't feel too left out of our neighbors' holidays and celebrations. St. Nicholas Day, celebrated on the sixth of December, was a holiday most looked forward to by all Christian children in Poland. One year, when my mother's good friend and a customer of the candy shop, Mrs. Szczygiel, was planning to take her three young daughters to a party featuring St. Nicholas, she invited me to go along.

The party took place in a large hall, at the top of which was a very big stage. A big red devil was jumping around on one side of the stage, holding a black pitchfork. I was standing in line along with other children, trying to keep my eyes off the scary devil. We all hoped to be able to get to sit on the kindly, bearded St. Nick's lap. The children exclaimed with joy when they opened the presents that St. Nick had given to them. Finally, my turn came. Hearing that I was a good girl, I too got a present. I excitedly opened my package. Inside were chocolates that looked very much like those that my father was making.

I had lots of friends in the neighborhood where we lived. We'd meet in the street for tag or hopscotch or jump rope, and we'd stay out until the streetlamps went on and our mothers called us in for dinner. I'd come indoors exhausted but happy from playing, with stories for my parents about who chased whom, and who got to be captain, and how many times I was able to skip rope without stopping or getting tangled up.

At the age of three I received a special present from my parents. It was a pink, ten-key, upright toy piano. I taught myself to play many children's songs, which until that time I was only able to sing. On the rare evenings when my mom and Tatu were able to leave their store early, I was happy to entertain them. Music would become one of the most important parts of my life, something I relied on during the hardest times.

My family was blessed with many good things, which made it hard to accept the reality of what was slowly starting to happen to us and to the rest of the Jewish people we knew. It's hard to recall exactly when it all began to change—the small ways in which we were discriminated against, the nasty, disapproving looks from people in the street, the feeling that we were somehow less than everyone else because of our religious beliefs.

As a toddler I got my first taste of anti-Semitism. My mother told me about it many years later. One day, when I didn't immediately respond to our housemaid's instructions, my mother overheard her calling me a Jew. Not understanding the implication of the word, and yet comprehending that she tried to insult me, I responded with "I am not; you are."

There is one specific day I can point to after which I'm certain nothing was quite the same: September 19, 1939. I had just turned five years old. When I woke up on that day I never could have imagined, even in my worst dreams, what was in store for my family and me. People on the balconies of the apartment building were yelling, and I ran to the kitchen in my pajamas to see what was going on.

"Tatu, what is it? What's all that noise?" I asked. He had a worried look on his face — I could tell because he got a little crinkle in his forehead when something disturbed him. "We're not sure," he said. "It seems like the Polish army is doing some kind of exercise." He scooped me up and stepped out onto the balcony to join my mother and the rest of the neighbors.

There was a loud buzzing in the sky, and so I had to stick my fingers in my ears. "There are so many of them," I said, taking one finger out for a moment to point at all the dark gray airplanes flying in formation above us. I looked at my parents. "I'm scared, Tatu!" I said. He hugged me tight and I buried my head in his neck. I would have buried myself beneath his skin if I could have. "It smells funny out here," I added, taking a finger out of my ear again to pinch my nose. The air had a thickness to it, an odor that was probably coming from the exhaust from all the planes.

Then the sirens blasted, and I could see the expressions on everyone's faces turn from confusion to terror. This wasn't an exercise. Germany was trying to invade our city. Then, above the noise of the sirens, we suddenly heard bombs falling and exploding. "Hurry!" one of the adults shouted, and within seconds we were all running to the basement to take shelter. The noise was deafening. I started to cry. I remember looking at my mother, and her face was completely drained of color. Tatu was still holding me, and my legs were bouncing up and down on his sides as he ran down the steps. My mother was right behind us. "Almost there," she said to me. "Then we'll be safe."

"But what's happening, what's happening?" was all I could keep repeating, over and over again.

In the basement, each family had a little cubicle used for storage, and we sat in ours as we listened to the terrible sounds of explosions and people screaming outside. My parents and I huddled together. It was cold and damp, and the closer we sat, the warmer we were. It was a depressing place to be, and I kept rubbing my nose because it smelled like mold. I tried hard to be brave, but my eyes kept filling with tears until I had no choice but to blink and let them fall down my cheeks. I felt like we might be in the basement forever and never be allowed to leave. What about all my dolls waiting for me upstairs? What about school? What about my friends?

The look on my face must have shown my parents that my mind was racing. "Let me tell you a story I know, a true one," Tatu said, pulling me onto his lap. "In heaven, there's a village just for dolls that can walk and talk. It's where all the dolls of all the children go when they get too old to be played with anymore or are broken and can't be fixed. They live in tiny

13

houses—blue, red, and yellow ones—with brown thatched roofs, and inside are tiny dishes and furniture. They are just like real, live dollhouses."

Tatu never lied to me, and so I had to believe what he said. "Really? How do you know?"

"Everyone knows," he said, "but you have to be five years old to find out, and since you just turned five I thought you might like to know."

I looked at my mother, who was nodding her head in agreement.

"It's true," she said. "When I was five my father told me the same story, and I was just as shocked as you are now, but it's true."

I started to smile. "How wonderful," I said. "So the doll I had last year, the one that was worn so thin that the stuffing was coming out and I finally had to give her up, she'll be there?"

"Yup," Tatu said. "She'll be there, except she won't be all tattered like she was. She'll be brand-new."

I was so happy to learn about the doll village that I completely forgot where we were. All I could think about was how much fun it would be to see the dolls alive, walking and talking.

The air raids went on for days. In between them, we went up to the apartment to use the bathroom and get some food. As strange as it might seem, I got used to the sound of the bombs and became bored sitting in the basement with all the adults. The only other child down there was a two-year-old boy named Ludush, and of course he wasn't much of a playmate. On the day we first used the basement as an air-raid shelter, Ludush had a runny nose and a cold. His parents had a hard time keeping him calm, and he'd run around, ducking behind walls, playing hide-and-seek. "Ludush," his mother would yell at him, "there are too many of us down here for you to be running around like this! You're annoying everyone!"

"It's okay," my mother said. "He's just a baby. People understand." People did understand, but at the same time it strained everyone's nerves because we were in such tight quarters. Even though we were able to go upstairs to wash, the basement had started to take on the stench of sweat.

But anyone who became annoyed with Ludush even for a moment still felt awfully guilty, because a few days later he lay listlessly on his mother's lap, burning with fever. There was no doctor in the building and no doctor nearby. "What can I do?" his mother cried. "I'm afraid he's going to die if I don't do something, but there doesn't seem to be anything to do! I can't just sit here and watch him get sicker and sicker, but I can't take him outside because then we might get killed by the bombs!" No one knew what to say. No one wanted to give her any advice, either, because it was a decision the adults knew she needed to make on her own. Finally, with an air of determination, she picked him up and, with bombs falling all around her, carried him to the hospital down the street. We later learned that Ludush had scarlet fever, a serious and contagious disease that children get. I was lucky I didn't catch it.

After several days, the bombing ended. When the German army marched into Lvov, the lives of all the Jewish people became terrible. I stopped going to school, and we had to wear white armbands with a blue Star of David on them. You could get into trouble if your armband was dirty, and so my mother found these funny-looking plastic ones for us to wear instead, so she could wipe them clean. I didn't like the way the band looked on my arm — it was quite unattractive — plus they'd crinkle the fabric of my dresses because I'd sweat underneath them. I'd plead with my mother. "Why do I have to wear it here?" I'd say. "Can't I wear it on my wrist so that it doesn't ruin my dress?"

For this, my mother had no patience. "What would you rather have happen, Luncia? Would you rather have a few wrinkles in your dress during the day, which I can press out when you get home, or risk getting in serious trouble for not obeying the law?" Even though I was still very young, my mother always spoke to me like an adult, never like a baby, which I eventually grew to appreciate very much. But at that moment all I could do was sulk as she attached the band in the proper place. One late evening I heard screams. I heard people calling for help in Polish and German. These voices were interspersed with shouts in the Ukrainian language. I had never heard more than a few people screaming at once. The neighborhood we lived in had mostly three-story-high buildings. These screams of terror came from one of the buildings. It seemed like the words "Help" were pounding drums. I asked my mother, who had come into the bedroom, where I was laying in my bed, too scared to move, and she explained what was happening.

She told me about the Ukrainian nationalists, mostly farmers from the surrounding villages of Lvov, who were coming in hordes into the city. They were barging into Jewish homes. They were armed with huge bats and sticks with which they were hitting people and smashing their possessions to bits. The sound of breaking furniture and glass filled the evening air. Since the calls for help came from Jewish homes, the German police didn't respond.

The next morning my mother and I went across the street to visit one of her friends, Miss Manya, whose apartment was broken into the night before by one of those evil hordes. There were broken glasses and dishes all over the floor. Miss Manya was showing her bruised legs to my mother. Her arms were covered with red, ugly welts. Her elderly father was sitting in a daze and stared into space. An open wound on his head was oozing blood.

While my mother was trying to help the injured people, I was telling myself that the horrible scene in front of my eyes was only a nightmare. Finally, the reality of the situation penetrated my mind. I began to cry. Noticing my great distress, my mother took me by my hand and walked me out of the apartment.

From that day on I was afraid to go to bed in the evening. Even though I let my mother get me into my pajamas, I refused to lie down. On many such evenings Tatu put my head on his shoulder and tried to comfort me by saying, "Do not be scared, Luncia, close your eyes. Those bandits will not come to our house. I will tell you a nice story."

But every day it seemed as if we had a new rule to follow. First, families were told to gather all their gold and silver and bring it to the synagogue. My mother took off her gold bracelet and Tatu his gold watch, and my mother took the silver candlesticks off the mantel and Tatu put all the silverware from the drawer inside a blue velvet case. They piled everything on the dining-room table, ready to go. It looked like we were getting ready to move.

I watched my parents as they did this, and I could see the sad looks on their faces, which made me feel awful. It's hard to see your parents upset, because they're the ones who are supposed to be strong all the time. Plus they barely spoke to each other. This was rare, because they were always talking or arguing over silly things, something I think they actually enjoyed, because they'd always end up smiling and laughing soon after they started. Now, every so often one of them would say, "Uh-huh, I guess so." A deep sigh followed, or else a comment about something that had to be given away, such as, "Those were my great-grandma's candlesticks, and my mother used them every Friday night. I can't believe I'll never see them again." My parents did what they had to do with a look of defeat and despair, and I suppose neither of them wanted to think about those moments any more than they had to.

Then everyone had to turn in their furs. The Germans said they would be used to line the uniforms of soldiers fighting in Russia, where it was very cold. Off came the gray rabbit fur from my favorite dark red winter coat and hat. They looked so plain without the trim that I didn't want to wear them anymore. As I watched my mother remove the fur, I stomped around the apartment, feeling that it wasn't fair to have to give up something that was mine to a faraway stranger.

"It's for the soldiers," my mother said. "Sometimes in life, we have to think of the needs of others, even if it's hard to do."

"I suppose so," I said, knowing that she was right but not liking it one bit. My mother said that she would sew on strips of silk from an old skirt of hers to make my coat fancier, and this made me feel a little better.

After the fur went the furniture. The Nazis would come into Jewish homes and force the Jews to carry what the Germans wanted to trucks waiting in the street.

One day Tatu was heading home. He was carrying a most precious commodity: a package of salt that he was able somehow to buy. Suddenly he was stopped by a uniformed German, who was standing next to a large truck. "You will carry the furniture," said the man, pointing at the building to the side of them. The Nazi grabbed the little package my father was holding and threw it into the cab of the truck. Tatu went upstairs and entered an apartment through an open door. He went into the kitchen and tried to take out a small table. A woman was sitting nearby. Seeing what my father was attempting to do, she started to cry, saying "Don't take my table. That is the only one I have."

After a moment, Tatu realized that he couldn't be an accomplice to this project.

He went out to the street, deciding to try a novel approach: to speak to the Nazi man to man. "Sir," he said, "it is really getting late. My wife will worry, wondering why I am not home yet. Do you mind if I go?"

In that moment, the Nazi forgot that he was talking to a Jew. He reached into the cabin of the truck, handed the little package to my father, and said, "Go ahead."

Later that evening my parents found out that after the furniture was delivered to a warehouse, all the men who carried furniture were shot. The driver of the truck, whom my father dared to approach as one human being to another, was the executioner.

My parents had had a beautiful walnut dining-room set made for us by a neighborhood shop just before the war began. He'd taken me to watch Mr. Baum, the carpenter, polish the wood to shiny perfection, and Mr. Baum would ask me if I could see my reflection in the door of the breakfront.

"How do you get it so shiny?" I'd always ask him, and he'd roll up his sleeve and show me his arm.

"See this?" he'd say, pointing to a muscle just below his elbow. "This is how I do it." He'd squeeze his hand

and I'd watch the muscle pop up and down. "My father had the same muscle in the same place, and so did my grandfather. Except mine is bigger," he'd say with a wink.

Tatu, upset, took ashes and rubbed down the table and chairs to make them look ugly so the Germans wouldn't want them. He had ash all over his face. I went over to him with a towel to wipe it off. "I hope they don't take it," I told him to try to make him feel better.

"Me, too," he said. "They're expensive pieces, ones I was hoping would be in our family for generations to come." He stood up to take stock of his progress and turned to my mother. "You know what? I don't care how much we get for it. I'd rather see it go to a family we know than to the Nazis. If we can't keep it, it would make me feel better knowing that a loving family was sitting down to dinner at it every night and enjoying it."

"If that's what you want to do, I'll ask the Christian family downstairs if they want it," my mother said.

She went downstairs and came back up a few minutes later, saying that they'd take it, and my father went down to negotiate a price. He ended up selling the furniture for next to nothing, but it gave Tatu peace of mind, which he said meant more than the money.

We also weren't allowed to lock our doors anymore. Late one afternoon, my mother was preparing supper for Tatu, and I was sitting in my usual spot on the red chair next to the window, when a German soldier burst in through the door. My mother gasped at the sight of him, my eyes got wide, and I froze.

"Give me all your gold and silver right now. Now!" he barked at my mother. "And you'd better not tell me you don't have any, because I know you must have saved some somewhere."

"But we've already given it all up," my mother pleaded. "We have nothing left."

Then the soldier stomped over to me. He smelled like a mix of cologne, cigarettes, and liquor. I thought for sure he would kill me, but before I even knew what was happening he reached his hands into the two pockets of my skirt to see what was in them. When he didn't find anything, he turned to my mother. "Fine," he said. "Give me that pot on the stove. It must be worth quite a bit."

We didn't have a lot of money for food at that point and so there were only potatoes cooking, but I was really looking forward to eating them. I watched my mother put the half-boiled potatoes on a plate and wash the pot for the soldier. When he left, my mother said she'd heard that the Germans needed metal for war materials.

When Tatu came home and my mother told him what had happened, he said, "It's just an excuse. They're making excuses so they can take everything they can from us. It's not going to stop with gold and silver and pots. It's never going to stop until they've taken everything—maybe even our lives." He whispered this last part to my mother, so that I wouldn't hear. But I heard, and it terrified me.

With every day that passed, our lives became harder, and scarier. At night when my mother and Tatu thought I was asleep, I'd hear them talk about the killings that were happening every day. Germans would randomly ask people for identification papers in the street, and they would pick out the Jews and shoot them. Hearing this made me sweat uncontrollably, and in the morning my pillow and sheet would be damp and cold. I wished I really had been sleeping.

Next, all the Jewish people were ordered to live in a certain area of the city. We were lucky in that we already lived in that part. Because we had a large apartment, we had to share it with two other families. I already felt how much less we had in our lives compared to only a few months before, and so when my mother told me that I had to move out of my room, I got upset. "It took me so long to get it decorated just the way I like it, and now strangers will have it!"

"It's because our bedroom—mine and Tatu's—is bigger, and we want to give ourselves as much space as possible," my mother said. "It's the best thing for all of us." I wasn't sure I agreed. I'd rather have had less space and not have my things disturbed. I sulked for a while, but after watching my mother work so hard to set up my room for our new tenants, I helped her. At least then I'd be able to pack my things away knowing what I put with what. My mother set up a small electric stove in one of the apartment's bathrooms, which the other families also used as a kitchen.

At least I had a new live-in playmate. Henio, who

came with his parents and his grandmother, was a year older than me. We mostly played tag in the hallways of the apartment building because it wasn't safe for us anymore to be outside on our own.

At night everyone who lived in the building would gather in our kitchen to discuss the war, and Henio and I would sit underneath the windows and listen. It was comforting to have all the people in our house. It almost felt like when we used to have big family parties and my mother would try to get everyone to sit in the living room because she thought it was a nicer place to entertain, but everyone always ended up sitting in the kitchen. "Why," she'd say, "why do we always end up in the kitchen when we have such lovely furniture in here?" Now she couldn't say that because most of our furniture was gone.

But during these discussions the conversation was a lot more serious than it had been at our parties. One night everyone was talking about something that was so frightening to me that Henio and I could barely breathe as we listened. There were rumors of an *akzia*, which is Polish for deportation. This meant that the Germans would come to take a large group of people away to kill them. The adults thought that an *akzia* would be happening in a few days. The worst part was that the first *akzia* in Lvov was to take away children. Henio and I looked at each other when we heard this, but neither of us could think of anything to say, so all we did was hug each other. At last, one of us spoke. "At least we'll be together," Henio said.

"That's true," I said, "but I still don't want to be without my parents."

"Me, neither," he said. "Let's try not to think about it for now."

But for the next few days, all we could do was think about it. Henio and I were too upset and anxious to do anything except sit by the window and stare outside. Winter was on its way, and all the leaves had fallen off the trees. Every so often one of us would say something, but we didn't have the focus or the energy to hold a very long conversation.

Tatu had already started to build a hiding place for Henio and me. He took off the bathroom door and put the white wardrobe my mother used in the kitchen in front of the opening. Then he cut a hole in the back of the wardrobe so Henio and I could quickly slip inside to hide in the bathroom. My mother hung a lot of clothing in the wardrobe in front of the hole.

I woke up on the morning of the *akzia* to the sound of women and children shrieking outside. I knew I had to get out of bed, but I felt so dizzy and nauseous I could barely move. Henio was already up and sitting at the kitchen table with his parents. I could tell he'd been crying.

"Hi," I said to him. He nodded and gave a little wave of his hand.

"How are you doing?" I asked, trying to get a little more out of him. But he just shrugged his shoulders, so I figured it was best to leave him alone.

Our mothers had prepared a bag of bread and a jar of water for each of us in case we were discovered and taken away.

"Okay, kids, it's time," Tatu said, trying to keep his emotions in check. "In you go," and he helped us climb in. As we pushed our way through the clothes and into the dark bathroom, I started to shake. Henio grabbed my hand and squeezed it, and I squeezed his back. "I can't stop shaking!" I whispered to him. "And my teeth! They're chattering so loudly! Can you hear?"

"A little. Here, bite on this," he said, handing me a shirt he pulled off a hanger. "You won't be able to chatter if you're biting."

The screams from outside seemed to be getting closer to our building.

Suddenly, there was the sound of heavy boots on the wood floor in the kitchen. Henio and I squeezed each other's hands tighter, and I bit down as hard as I could on the cloth. Everything felt as if it were spinning around me — it was bad with my eyes open, but it was even worse when I closed them. We heard a booming, deep voice ask my parents where I was. I remembered that there was a picture of me wearing a pair of cute striped pajamas hanging on the wall, and no one had thought to take it down. *No!* I thought. *The man is going to notice it and start asking them about me!* There was nothing that would have given him any idea to ask about Henio. And in fact the man did ask about the picture. Then in a strong, emotional voice I heard Tatu say, "She was already taken away," and the Nazi, who must have been looking at the picture, said, "You had a pretty little girl."

We thought he would leave after that, but all of a sudden Henio and I saw the beam of a flashlight shining through the tiny crack between the thick, carved door frame and the wardrobe. I squeezed my eyes shut and held my breath, and the dizziness got even worse. I heard Henio fighting to hold his breath. I was sure that in the next moment the soldier would shove the wardrobe away from the door and find Henio and me sitting there on the floor, and our lives would be over. But then his footsteps started to move away. A few minutes later, it sounded as if someone was opening the wardrobe. To our relief, it was Tatu, who came to tell us that it was safe for us to come out. He looked drained.

"I feel sick, Tatu," I said. "I feel like if I get up I'm going to fall down and faint." Tatu and Henio helped me out slowly, and Tatu sat me down on a kitchen chair.

"Here," he said, handing me a glass of water with a little sugar and salt in it. "Drink. It'll make you feel better."

Within a few minutes, I did. Before I got up from the chair, Henio had already gone back to sleep, and I thought it'd be a good idea if I did the same. In the few moments before I drifted off, I thought about how close I'd come to getting taken away, and probably to dying as well. How was it that I survived? How was it that the Nazi didn't find us, and I was still there in the apartment with my parents? The thoughts kept getting more and more jumbled in my head, until I finally exhausted myself even more and fell asleep.

A few days later we heard rumors of another *akzia*. This time it was for the elderly. My grandma Bela, along with all the other older women in Lvov, tried to buy black hair dye so they'd look younger, but my grandmother came home from the store empty-handed. "It was all gone—all gone by the time I got there, and I'd waited in line three hours," she said. "What should I do?" Luckily, she escaped capture that time, but would eventually be taken away.

Two weeks later, there was another *akzia*. This one was for *all* Jews. Since my parents still had the keys to their candy shop, they decided we would hide there. My uncle Hirsch, my aunt Clara, and my cousins, Benny, who was eleven years old, and Fancia, who was ten, came with us.

We snuck into the store in the middle of the night. Tatu was able to move the heavy iron gates, and we quickly went inside. A very cold winter had come early, and the store wasn't heated.

"I'm freezing," I said to my mother.

"Try to think warm thoughts," she replied. "Pretend you're at the park on a sunny day and it's so hot you have to take off your jacket. Sometimes mind over matter can work if you try hard enough."

I tried to do it, but it was no use. I'd just have to deal with being cold, and that was the end of it. There were no blankets or pillows for us to use, and the tile floor was colder than the air. We all tried to sleep as best we could, but Uncle Hirsch was sick and had a bad cough. At one point close to dawn, Fancia got up and walked over to her father. She took off her coat and covered him with it. When morning finally came, I got up and looked through the cracks in the gate to see what was happening in the street.

"Oh, no, what's going on?" I asked. My cousins were the first to join me at the window. It was horrible. Dozens of the open-top trucks that farmers used to transport horses were lined up along Grodecka Street, where all the businesses were. They were filled with Jewish people and were headed toward the railroad station. Adults sat with their heads hanging low, and little children clutched their mothers' skirts.

Then I felt Tatu's hand on my shoulder. "Luncia, Ben, Fancia," he said to us in a hushed voice, "you shouldn't be watching this. It's not good for you to see. It'll only make you more upset. Come to the back of the store."

After the *akzia*, we left the store and went back to the apartment building, and for a few days things were quiet. It was like we'd cleared another hurdle, survived another test. But before a week passed, there was another *akzia*. I heard my mother talking to Tatu about having me stay with someone Christian so I wouldn't have to hide. As much as I didn't want to be separated from my parents, I knew I'd be more comfortable at someone's house. "I can ask Mrs. Zofia," she said to Tatu. "I'm sure she wouldn't mind. It would just be for a day." Tatu agreed that it was a good idea.

When my mother took me to Mrs. Zofia's early the next morning, I didn't want to say good-bye to her. But then Mrs. Zofia's daughter, Kathy, who was close to my age, came over to say hello, and suddenly it felt as if I was being dropped off for a playdate, so I gave my mother a quick hug and a wave.

Kathy had dark red hair that was styled in braids, and when she walked, the braids bounced up and down and the sweet smell of her shampoo was in the air all around her.

She was eager to start playing right away, and seeing her bright, happy face made me feel happy, too. She didn't have any idea I was Jewish, of course, and came up with an idea for a game. "Let's go to the window and count all the Jews passing our street," she said. This made me feel sick to my stomach.

"But, er, um, how are we supposed to know who's Jewish and who isn't?" I asked.

"Silly," she said, "we can count the people with the armbands."

At that moment, it felt as if the armband I usually wore was still attached to my arm, and my heart jumped for a second until I remembered it wasn't there.

For what seemed like hours, I had to play this game with Kathy.

"Okay, I'm bored with this," she said. "Let's do something else." I nodded furiously. "I have some nice dolls we can play with. Would you like that?"

"Oh, I love dolls!" I said. "Yes, let's play with them."

As we dressed her dolls in new dresses, one of their neighbors stopped by. She was busy talking with Mrs. Zofia but kept turning her head to look at us. Then she came over and asked Kathy to introduce me. "Who's this?" she asked. "Is she a good friend of yours?"

"Oh," said Kathy, "I've actually never met her before. She's the daughter of someone my mother used to work with. Her name is Luncia."

The neighbor stuck out a hand to introduce herself. "Nice to meet you," she said, and I stuck out my hand and gave a slight nod. I was too afraid to say anything that would reveal who I was and why I was there, so I just nodded politely.

Early the next morning, Mrs. Zofia took me back to my parents' house. "I'm sorry," she told my mother, "but my neighbor said that Luncia looked really sad and then asked if she was a Jewish girl. I had to lie and tell her no, that she was just shy and was just getting over a cold and wasn't her normal, perky self. But I can't do you this favor again. I'm afraid to get reported."

"I'm sorry that happened," my mother said, thanking her for taking me in. Luckily, the *akzia* had already ended.

About two weeks later, the worst news of all came. All Jews were ordered to leave their homes and move into the ghetto. The ghetto was a small, run-down area just outside the city. It was surrounded by a tall fence and guarded by Nazi soldiers. No one was allowed to leave the ghetto unless the Nazis decided they could.

Tatu and our next-door neighbor left right away to go find us a place to live inside the ghetto. Even though we were devastated that we'd have to move there, my parents knew that if they didn't find us a place we'd have to live on the streets. Tatu came home later that night relieved to have found us a small room in a tiny two-room house. "What does it look like?" my mother and I asked him at almost the same time. He'd barely taken off his coat. "Well, it really isn't much," Tatu told us. "It's very small, and we're going to be sleeping in an even tighter space than we have now. The toilet isn't indoors—it's outside, in the back, and so it's called an outhouse. We're really going to have to pare down our possessions to the basic essentials. We won't have room for anything extra."

We left for the ghetto two days later. All we took with us were three folding cots, a small table, and some clothing. I wasn't allowed to bring any of my toys, even my favorite doll with her white carriage. I cried about it from the minute I woke up until afternoon, but when Uncle Hirsch came barging through our door and into the kitchen just as Tatu was putting all our things into a wheelbarrow, I stopped crying.

"I—I," he stammered, "I . . . something terrible happened," Uncle Hirsch said. He looked disheveled, and his hair was stringy and greasy.

"Sit, sit," my mother said. "What is it?" she asked.

"Is everyone okay?" Tatu added.

"No, it's terrible," my uncle began. "Earlier today the Nazis came to the apartment and ordered us—just me and Clara—downstairs to one of the waiting trucks. Clara was crying and grabbed Fancia and Ben and wouldn't let go of them, but the soldier pried them out of her arms. Then he grabbed the two of us by the clothes on our backs and marched us downstairs and shoved us into a truck with other adults . . ." His voice trailed off and he started crying again. Tatu put a hand on his shoulder.

Then Uncle Hirsch composed himself and continued. "I could still hear the kids' voices yelling and crying after us upstairs, even from the street," he said. "It was awful to just leave them like that. The truck drove us out of town and into the woods and stopped at the side of a road. Everyone was told to get out and run in single file toward a clearing in the distance. When it was my turn to run, Clara, who was standing behind me, said, 'Don't run! Another minute to live!' But as I moved forward, I noticed some bushes on the side of the road, and instead of running to the clearing I ran toward them. I managed to not get shot, but Clara . . ." His voice trailed off again, and he started to sob uncontrollably. Then the rest of us started to cry, too. We tried to console him and think of the right things to say, but nothing seemed right.

"Go home and be with the children," Tatu said to his brother. "They need you right now. You just lost a wife, but they just lost a mother. You're all they've got. We'll meet up together once we all get to the ghetto."

Uncle Hirsch nodded and we walked out of the apartment together. Tatu suddenly remembered one thing that he didn't want to leave behind. There was a box covered with green-and-white printed paper that held all our family photographs. He went back in to grab it, then gently closed the door, and we were on our way.

We walked to the ghetto with other families, many of whom we knew and talked with along the way. I was leaving my whole world behind, the only place I'd ever lived. Would I see it again? I said good-bye to every house and every street we passed and tried to burn an image of all of my favorite places into my mind. I breathed in deeply when we passed the bakery and the pastry shop. Looking at my parents' faces and seeing how they fixed their eyes on things longer than usual, I knew that they were doing the same.

After walking for two hours and becoming exhausted, we reached the ghetto. Compared to the lively streets and well-kept houses in Lvov, the ghetto looked dingy and gray. People were sitting on the sidewalks, and mothers with crying children latched onto them begged for food. There were stray cats and dogs everywhere, adding to the chaos. The air had an acidic smell, like a mix of chemicals and urine.

"I want to go home," I said to my mother. "It's awful here."

"I'm afraid this is home for now," my mother said. "You're right—it is awful. No human being should have to live in these conditions."

Finally, we found the tiny house. It was painted white, but the paint was badly chipped. Three steps in front led up to a small porch. The door made a loud *thwap* when it closed behind us. Our room was even smaller than the kitchen in our old apartment. In the back was a window, and through it I could see the outhouse. We dropped our things in the corner. It was getting dark, and so Tatu started opening up our cots. There was barely room to walk around them.

"It's so, so small," I said to my mother. "I'm a small girl and I can't even walk around the beds without bumping my knees. I'll have bruises all over them all the time!"

"Let's go out for a walk," my mother said. "We can leave Tatu here to set things up and when we come back it'll look better than it does now."

We went outside and walked around the back of the house, and my mother pointed out a huge barn in the far end of the backyard. There was a lot of movement going on inside, and then I realized that it was filled with peoples' living spaces, on the ground and in the hayloft. I thought about how animals had lived there, and now these people were living like animals. "See," my mother said. "No matter how bad you think you have it, there's always someone who has it worse. Don't you feel sorry for them?" I nodded my head. It made me feel lucky to at least have our little room.

When I went back inside, our neighbors had arrived. "Nice to meet you," all of the adults said to one another, shaking hands. There were four people in their family, so we were seven all together. The only other child was a boy named Siunio. He was quite a bit younger than me, and so I felt it was my duty, as the older girl, to initiate a hello. I gave a little wave, but he ran and hid himself behind his mother's skirts. I had a feeling he wouldn't be much of a playmate.

Uncle Hirsch, Fancia, Benny, and our grandma were lucky enough to find someplace to stay, too. They lived in a small attic of a house a few streets away, and I'd go visit them whenever I could. There were four long flights of rickety stairs to climb, and when I got to the top, it took me a little while before I could have a conversation with anyone, because I had to catch my breath.

My favorite thing to do there was to look at pictures. Grandma would get photographs from our family in America and she'd always make sure to point everyone out to me. I was only allowed to hold them with clean hands, and so the first thing I had to do when I got to the attic was wash them.

"Be careful not to put your fingerprints on the

pictures," she would say. "You have to hold them by the edges, like this," and she'd show me the proper way to do it.

"Who's this tall man with a beard?" I'd ask her. "What about this girl in the lovely dress?" Or "Where are they in this picture?" These were my usual questions. The photos were of my cousins Izzy, Leon, and Helen, and my uncle Joseph. There was also cousin David, Uncle Abe and Aunt Ida, and Uncle Benny and Aunt Rebecca, who all lived in New York.

In the ghetto, hunger was our daily companion. The little bit of bread that my mother was able to buy with the coupons that the Germans alotted to the Jews was made partially from sawdust. We didn't mind its horrible taste. If only the rations were a little bigger!

Whoever had a little money and was able to sneak out of the ghetto bought food on the outside and brought it into the ghetto in their pockets. It was primarily bread. One street was unofficially designated as the "black market." I can still hear in my mind the voices of the few sellers of bread calling out: "Who wants a whole, who a half, who a quarter loaf of bread?"

As a rule the Germans wouldn't come into the ghetto to "take away" any Jewish people if it wasn't the day of an *akzia.* However, some uniformed Germans would stroll into the ghetto just to "sightsee."

On such occasions, when one spotted a German, he or she would say the word *sechs* in a loud whisper. People would pass the word around, and in a few minutes the street would become totally empty. *Sechs* means the number six in German. I really don't know why this word was used as a warning.

Even though all the Jews of Lvov now lived in the ghetto, there were still *akzias.* Tatu and Siunio's father would stay up late at night and talk about the best place for us to hide. Finally, they decided that it would be under the porch. Tatu cut a hole in the back of a credenza and moved it in front of the entry to our hiding place. To get inside, we'd have to crawl in through the credenza. It took them about a week to dig out a space big enough to fit all seven of us.

A few days after the hiding place was finished, my mother woke me up very early. "Quickly," she said in a hurried whisper. "It started earlier than we expected. We all have to hide right now!"

I pulled on my clothes as fast as I could. It was rumored that this *akzia* was to last for several days. As we started to climb in, my mother noticed

Miss Manya, one of our neighbors, standing nearby. Somehow she had found out about the hiding place.

"Can I come in, is there room for me?" she asked. "I don't have anyplace else to go. Please!" she pleaded. There was barely enough room for the rest of us, but the adults decided that they couldn't turn her away.

We squeezed together so tightly that we could hardly breathe. It was very hot in there, so I thought it strange that Miss Manya had her coat over her shoulders. Soon we heard heavy footsteps above us. It reminded me of the last time I hid, with Henio. I almost started to cry, but I decided I needed to set an example for Siunio so I bit my lip and held back my tears. After a while the Nazis left, probably thinking that we'd already been taken.

Once it was dark outside, we silently snuck back into the room. The next morning we returned to our little cave. Because we were basically hiding outside, we could easily hear what was going on in the street. We heard the trucks idling at the curb and people's cries as the Nazis put them inside the trucks. All of a sudden, we heard two familiar voices. They belonged to Fancia and Ben. "Uncle! Aunt! Luncia!" they cried.

When my mother saw that I was about to call out

after them, she covered my mouth with her hand and whispered in my ear, "We can't, Luncia. We can't have them. It's impossible. There just isn't enough room." Soon the sound of their voices faded.

Tears started streaming down my face at the thought of my cousins being taken away. I remembered something that had happened with Benny a few days ago. While I was visiting my cousin, he motioned to follow him into the corner of the room and said that he wanted my advice on something important. Straightening out my skinny body and looking at me with eyes that were wise beyond his twelve years, Benny said, "My dad gave me a few coins. I have a choice. I can either buy a cookie, which is delicious, or an egg, which is very healthy. What should I do?" I was very proud to be asked such a question by my very smart cousin. Not really waiting for my answer, Benny said: "I want to live and be healthy, so I will buy an egg." I couldn't believe he would soon die.

My mother put her other palm on my forehead, stroking it and rocking me to try to calm me down. Finally, I was calm enough and she removed her hand from my mouth.

"How could this be happening?" I whispered to her. I shook my head back and forth and almost started to cry again. "What if our family gets taken? What will we do?"

My mother looked as if she was feeling exactly like I was. "I don't know, Luncia. We won't know anything until morning, so for now try to get some sleep."

The *akzia* continued late into the night, and so we didn't leave the hiding place to go back to our room. In the morning, it was over. As we crawled out, we discovered why Miss Manya had her long coat with her. It was to hide her little dog. Had the dog started to bark or whine, we might have been found. Tatu was the most upset of all.

"How could you have done that, risking all our lives with that dog!" he screamed. "What if he had barked? Dogs bark! They don't know any better! Then we would all have been dead! And we took you in even though there wasn't room to begin with!"

All Miss Manya could do was look at her feet. "I'm sorry," she said. "I love this dog like a child. I couldn't just leave him out in the street."

Tatu shook his head and walked away in disgust. It was hard for me not to think that if we hadn't let her in there would have been enough room for my cousins. I became so angry I nearly screamed at her as well. We had survived another *akzia* and escaped death yet again, but I feared the same wasn't true for the rest of our family.

The moment we crawled out of the hole, we hurried to check up on Grandma, Uncle Hirsch, and my cousins. I ran ahead of my parents, and they were a minute or two behind. By the time I got to the top of the attic steps, I was even more out of breath than usual. "Oh, no! No!" I screamed when I got to the top. The room was empty. I ran back downstairs, tears streaming, and got to the bottom just as my parents arrived. "It's empty! Mother, Tatu, they're gone. Gone! There's no one there!"

The three of us huddled together and wept. A man who lived in the room next to our relatives came out when he heard us crying. Through a crack in the door of a closet he'd been hiding in, he had seen the whole family being taken away.

We walked back to our little room with our hearts heavy. Now it was just the three of us. "We're alone," Tatu said. "But I suppose even in our sadness we need to be thankful for what we do have, which is one another." My mother and I nodded in agreement. It was true. As far as we knew, the only family we had left lived in America.

No one but people lucky enough to have a job on the outside were allowed to leave the ghetto. Tatu was one of them, and so was Siunio's father. Every morning, just as the sun was coming up, they would stand in line with the other men who had "Useful Jew" ID cards, waiting for the guards to wave them through the ghetto's gate.

After we'd been living in the ghetto for about three months, I overheard Tatu telling my mother and the other adults a story after he came home from work one evening. "I ran into Mrs. Szczygiel, this morning," he began. The Szczygiel family had been friends with my parents since I was a baby and had been loyal customers of our store, Sarotina. "She told me how glad she was to see me alive," my father continued. "Then she hugged me and said, 'Isaac, you and Barbara will probably not survive the war. Let me take Luncia. I'll raise her as my daughter.'"

I gasped when I heard this. How could my parents consider giving me to someone else? We should be together! How could this possibly be the best thing for me? When my mother heard this, she started to cry. I wasn't sure if she was crying because she was sad to be separated from me or if she was happy that I had a place to go. Maybe it was both.

"How would we even get Luncia out of the ghetto?" she asked Tatu.

"I don't know," Tatu said, and then he told her the story of what had happened before he ran into Mrs. Szczygiel. It was still dark outside, and it was very cold. As he got near the gate, he noticed that the man walking in front of him was shivering. When the guard asked the man for his ID card, the man reached into his pocket to get it out, but because he was so cold his hand was shaking and he couldn't get it out quickly. The guard had no patience.

"Shoot him," he said to the other guard.

My father heard the shot and saw the man fall in front of him.

"See if he has his card, just for the fun of it." The guard reached into the man's pocket and pulled out the card. "Well," the guard said, "that man had no luck."

"I saw a man killed when I was standing in line last week," Siunio's father said. He said he had just gotten there when he saw a guard yelling at a man near the gate. The guard yelled "Jew!" to the two guard dogs that always sat there, and they attacked and killed the man.

After hearing these two stories, I was terrified by the idea of having to be smuggled past the guards and their dogs, but my parents were intent on getting me out so I could live with the Szczygiels. The next morning, my mother dressed me in dark clothing that would blend in with Tatu's dark gray coat. "Mother, what if this doesn't work?" I asked her in a million different ways. I had tons of "what if" questions that morning that I kept rattling off one after another, but all she kept saying to me was, "You have to believe, Luncia. You have to believe that you will live. That's the only thing you can do."

Mother told me to hold on tight to Tatu's leg, and I wrapped myself around him. Tatu slipped on his big coat, and my mother told Siunio's father to walk closely next to Tatu to help keep me hidden. My mother bent down and kissed me all over my face. "Will I ever see you again?" she kept saying in between bursts of tears. I didn't know what to say to this. Tatu said that we needed to leave quickly, and then we were on our way.

It seemed as if we were walking forever. Not being able to see from under Tatu's coat, I didn't even know if we had passed the guards at the ghetto's gate. But just feeling the warmth of my father's body made me feel safe.

We finally arrived at the building where Tatu worked, narrowly escaping being discovered once again. When I got out from under his coat, we were in a large room with a lot of desks. Tatu introduced me to his coworkers, all of them Jewish people wearing white armbands with a Star of David on them.

Mrs. Szczygiel had promised Tatu that she would pick me up at three o'clock, but three came and went and she hadn't arrived. "Why hasn't she come, Tatu?" I asked. "Did she forget about me?"

"I don't think she would, Luncia," he said. "I honestly can't imagine why she wouldn't come. This was all her idea."

There was no telephone at the office so no one could call her. Jews weren't allowed to walk the streets, and no one would risk taking off an armband because if anyone was recognized and reported, the person identifying them would get a reward and the Jewish person would be shot dead on the spot.

By four, Tatu was really worried. The crinkle in his forehead started to come out. It was too dangerous to try to smuggle me back into the ghetto. Then Tatu had an idea. "Listen," he said to his coworkers, "tell me what you think of this. Do you know that young Christian boy, Robert, who works in the building?" Everyone shook their heads yes. "Well, I know that he's a sympathizer of the Jews. I've become friendly with him, and we've spoken about it several times. What do you think if I asked him to go speak with Mrs. Szczygiel to find out what's happened?" Everyone agreed that it was worth trying. Tatu ran downstairs to find Robert and brought him back upstairs to meet me. My father quickly explained the situation and without Tatu even having to ask, Robert offered to go to Mrs. Szczygiel's house to find out what had gone wrong.

After Robert left, everyone was very quiet. It was getting late and was almost time for Tatu and the other workers to return to the ghetto. Tatu paced back and forth, wringing his hands in desperation. Robert had been gone for more than an hour. Finally, he came back.

"Well? What the heck happened to her?" Tatu burst out the moment the boy returned. I don't think he could help himself, even though it came out sounding a bit rude.

"I told her that Luncia had been smuggled out of the ghetto and was waiting at the office," Robert told Tatu, "but then Mrs. Szczygiel said she'd changed her mind, that she didn't want to put her own family in danger by taking Luncia in. I listened to what she had to say, but then I told her that you couldn't risk taking Luncia back into the ghetto—that trying to smuggle her back in was too dangerous." Tatu had started to sweat heavily at this point. "So she was pacing back and forth and folding and unfolding her hands," Robert continued. "Then she closed her eyes and it looked as if she was saying a prayer, and when she opened her eyes she said, 'Since Luncia has already left the ghetto, tell her father that I'll definitely come to get her tomorrow.'"

"Thank God! Oh, thank God," Tatu said. "I don't know what we would have done." Everyone else looked relieved, too. But in the next moment, one by one, they all turned to look at me. Then Tatu said what they all must have been thinking—everyone except me, that is. "Luncia, you're going to have to stay here by yourself for the night," he said. "I can't stay with you."

"W-w-what do you mean?" I stammered. "I can't stay here alone! What am I supposed to do here by myself all night?"

"Just lie down on the table and try your best to go to sleep," Tatu said, hugging me close to his chest. "I'll be here first thing in the morning."

Everyone said good-bye, and the next minute I was alone in the huge office building. I tried to lie down on a desk, but it was uncomfortable. I tried the floor, but without a blanket or pillow, it wasn't much better. My heart started beating fast, and suddenly I was hot and cold at the same time, sweating and freezing all at once. It was so scary being in the huge, dark building, knowing I was completely alone. What if a Nazi came in and took me away? My parents would never know what had happened to me. I started to shake and couldn't manage to comfort myself, so I got up and walked around until I got tired, and then lay across a desk. I must have fallen asleep, because the next thing I knew, Tatu was standing in front of me with a wet rag, wiping the crusty tearstains off my face.

The afternoon passed quickly, and at three o'clock Mrs. Szczygiel arrived. I was glad she'd come but was miserable at the same time. Saying good-bye to my mother had been hard, but because I knew I was still going to be with Tatu I didn't get hysterical. All I could think when I was saying good-bye to Tatu was that I was never going to see my parents again. "Oh, Tatu!" I cried. "What am I going to do without you? I don't want to live anymore if I can't be with you!"

"Don't say that, Luncia," Tatu said. "You mustn't ever say that. You have to believe that you, your mother, and I will meet up again after this craziness is over, one way or another." He ran his hand across my cheek. I cried so hard that I could feel my face getting red and swollen.

Mrs. Szczygiel said it was time to go, and she led me outside. I had to bury my face in my hands. I didn't want to have to remember what Tatu looked like as I walked away.

Part II: In Hiding

It wasn't a long walk to the Szczygiels' apartment. Had I realized that it would be the last time I'd be outside for quite a while I would have tried to enjoy it more, but I was so exhausted from not sleeping well the night before that it was a blur.

When we got there, no one was home except Mrs. Szczygiel's mother, whom I came to call Babcia, which means grandma in Polish. Mr. Szczygiel and the three teenage daughters, Jasia, Hela, and Marysia, were at work.

Babcia took me right into the bedroom and told me to sit down on the small burgundy velvet couch in the corner. "You need to sit here and not move unless someone tells you to," she said in a stern voice. "Do you understand?" she asked. "It's very important that you understand this."

I nodded my head yes. It reminded me of being in school, sitting at my desk until our teacher told us to stand in a line, so I decided that I'd pretend that's what I was doing and maybe it would help me sit still.

Aside from the couch there was a large bed and a pretty dressing table. "And that dressing table in the corner," Babcia added, "I know it's going to be appealing to you to go over and play there, but you mustn't. It's too close to the window, and somone might see you from the apartment across the street." I shook my head again, thinking that she had read my mind—I did really want to go play at the dressing table.

Then I was given the rest of my rules. "You must stay in the bedroom," Babcia continued. "Use the small potty when you need to, and keep it under the bed. The bathroom is in the hallway and it's shared with the neighbors. If someone comes into the apartment, quickly crawl under the bed and hide behind suit-cases. Whisper whenever you speak, because the walls are thin, and if you talk in a normal voice someone will hear you. All right?"

"I understand," I said in what I thought was a soft voice.

"Shhh . . . that was too loud," Babcia said. "Quieter. You must speak even more quietly than that."

This certainly wasn't going to be like school.

Remembering to whisper wasn't hard from then on because I didn't really have anyone to talk to. But it was hard not to make any noise, because for the first few weeks I was there I sobbed uncontrollably. Every time I tried to keep the tears from coming, it was like a rock had gotten stuck in my throat, and it stayed stuck until I let the tears out. I had two handkerchiefs with me, and I'd cry into one and put it under the bed to dry, then cry into the other. I tried not to cry in front of anyone, especially Mrs. Szczygiel, because I didn't want her to think me ungrateful that she had taken me in. But one afternoon she came into the bedroom to get something out of the closet and she caught me crying. She came over and said, "Luncia, you mustn't cry. You're a very lucky little girl. Most of the people you know will not survive the war, but I'm going to raise you as my own daughter." I know she was trying to be kind, but what she said made me feel worse. I didn't want all the people I knew to die. What about Mother and Tatu, still in the ghetto? I might not ever see them again. I know I should have felt lucky, but I didn't.

I didn't have anything to keep my mind off my situation, either. There weren't any books to read, and no one thought to give me paper and a pencil to draw. I was too afraid to ask for it, so I just sat on the couch and told myself stories. Usually, they'd be fairy tales, and I'd go over them in my mind from beginning to end, trying to remember each detail. If I forgot something, I'd make myself go back and start from

The year is 1938, and I am four years old, at a mountain resort in Poland. I was a carefree child who loved to dance and sing.

With my parents, Barbara and Isaac Gamzer, at age four.

In Lvov, with my mother, age four.

Standing between my mom and dad
at my father's candy store, age four.

My kindergarten class (I am the sixth from the right in the last row). Every child in this photograph, except for myself, was killed in the Holocaust.

After the war, with my father in Krakow, Poland. My family and I had gone through so much and I was so happy to be with them again.

Age eleven, in Poland, after the war.

These were the socks I wore in hiding, from 1942-1944.

Almost a teenager in Munich, Germany.

With my friends from James Madison High School in
Brooklyn. I am in the center.

My high school graduation photo.

In New York at seventeen.

My wedding photo, with Jack Gruener.

In 1999, I traveled to Poland to visit Mrs. Oyak. It was an emotional reunion and I was so happy to see her again.

the very beginning. Maybe it was because my mother used to tell me fairy tales before bed, but sometimes during the day I'd catch myself dozing off. I'd lean my head back and before long Mrs. Szczygiel and Babcia's voices seemed very far away. What usually woke me up was the feeling of my head sliding down the wall.

It was hard to keep track of time passing because each day was the same. Every morning Mr. and Mrs. Szczygiel folded up the mattress that they slept on in the kitchen and put it in the closet. Jasia and Hela folded up the bed that pulled out from the burgundy couch and then fought to see who got to use the bathroom first. "You used it first yesterday!" one would scream. "No, you did," the other would scream back. Then, at the same time, the two would scream in unison, "Mommm!"

Marysia, Babcia, and I slept on the bed. They slept with their heads at the headboard, and I slept lengthwise at their feet, which was very uncomfortable because the two of them would unwittingly kick me during the night. They'd yell at me for twisting and turning, so I became afraid to move at all, or sneeze, or make any other noise.

When I got out of bed one morning, my head started to itch. Noticing my great discomfort, Babcia looked at me with suspicion. Then, with a knowing smile on her face, she told me that she suspected that I had head lice. She told me that when, a few days ago, Marysia had slept over at her friend's house, Marysia came home with those unwelcome guests in her hair. Since I slept next to her, some of the lice left her head and settled in mine.

Babcia immediately went into action. She asked me and Marysia to step into the kitchen, where she spread a large newspaper on the table. Asking us to bring our heads forward, she proceeded to comb our hair with a fine tooth comb. Suddenly I saw little creatures fall onto the paper. I had never seen a louse in my life and found it interesting to watch those creatures turn and squirm.

Babcia explained to me that she would have to rinse my head with kerosene to kill off the little eggs the lice had left behind in my hair. It worked.

Every morning, Babcia would order me to go sit on the couch and she and Marysia would make the bed, something I always thought Marysia hated me for because she thought making the bed was an annoying chore. Then Mr. Szczygiel and the girls would go off to work, and Mrs. Szczygiel would leave to go shopping. Babcia, who was the kindest to me, gave me some bread and tea-flavored water for breakfast. She'd stay in the apartment and clean until Mrs. Szczygiel came home from the market, and by then it would be dark outside, and dark in the apartment, too, because the lights weren't turned on until the rest of the family got home. Mrs. Szczygiel said keeping the lights on was expensive, and she said the same thing about the coal and wood for the ceramic stove in the bedroom.

I wasn't sure if my feet and hands got numb and itchy from the cold or from sitting still all day, but then I got my answer. When Babcia came with my tea water and bread one morning, she took one look at my hands and said, "Luncia! Your hands are red like beets! Take your socks off and let me see your feet!" So I took my socks off, and when she saw my feet she put her hand to her forehead and said, "Luncia! You have frostbite!" She ran to the kitchen and came back a few minutes later with a basin filled with boiled potato peels. "Here," she said. "Soak your feet and then your hands and the swelling will go down."

This is disgusting! I thought at first. But then I realized that I finally had something to play with. I mashed up the potato peels even more and made potato snow-balls, and I stacked them on one another as if I'd been making a real snowman.

Usually when Mrs. Szczygiel got home she and Babcia would gossip and argue in the kitchen. The door between rooms was kept closed. But sometimes, even though it was winter, the windows in the kitchen and the bedroom would be left open to air out the apartment and I could hear their voices coming from outside. Mrs. Szczygiel said it wasn't healthy for so many people to live in such a small space, which always made me feel bad because my presence certainly made it more crowded, and so she would throw open the windows to get all the germs out. Of course, there was a heated stove in the kitchen but no heat in the bed-room, so when she did this I spent the day freezing half to death.

I wasn't exactly sure what the two of them would gossip about. It usually sounded like, "And then so-and-so said to this one that she had never heard of such a thing. And then so-and-so said she couldn't believe it, either." I think they argued mostly because Babcia didn't like what Mrs. Szczygiel brought home from the market. I imagined that they were used to having meat a few times a week, like I had been, before the war. Sometimes I heard them arguing about "the girl," which I understood to be me. They were careful about what they said, not for my sake but because if anyone suspected that they were hiding me and they got reported to the Nazis by a neighbor, the whole family would be killed. And I would be killed, too.

But despite my sense of fear and sadness, I did like what happened after dinner. The three sisters sat in front of the mirror at their dressing table and talked about the fancy ladies they saw during the day on the street and took turns arranging different hairstyles for one another to wear the next day. They all had stick-straight hair, and wavy hair was in style. They couldn't buy rollers to curl it because rollers were expensive and money was tight during the war, and so they would fold a page of newspaper or magazine into a strip, wrap their hair around it, and secure it with a hairpin for the night. Watching them do this and listening to everything they said fascinated me. I tried not to let them know that I was eavesdropping, but when I heard their stories I'd imagine that their life was my life and that my mother had already put pins in my hair to keep my curls neat and that my dress for the next day—the royal blue velvet one with the ivory lace trim and scalloped edges on the bottom—was hanging on the hook next to the closet. And in the morning when I woke up, I'd go outside and see the ladies in their fancy clothes and hats as I walked to school.

Every day as I sat on my couch, the pretty dressing table taunted me. The wood was so dark and shiny that I could see the lace curtains reflected in it, like I used to see my face reflected in the dining room set Tatu had bought. The drawers had lighter wood details around the edges, and tiny pulls. The mirror was a big circle attached to the base in the back, so it seemed to be floating on top of the table, like a moon sitting on the horizon. All sorts of jars and bottles were arranged in front of the mirror, each a different size and shape, some colorful and some ordinary. There was a small stool tucked underneath the table that looked like a mushroom with a pink silk upholstered top. It was gorgeous.

Many days I was so bored I thought I might die. But one day in particular I felt as if I couldn't take it anymore, and so I tiptoed over to the dressing table, forgetting momentarily that I wasn't supposed to go near the window. I quietly slid the stool out from underneath the table and sat down and began opening the jars and putting different creams on my face. It was sort of like painting in school, except *I* was the canvas! Soon enough I tired of it and retreated to the couch. Somehow it seemed as if the girls had more fun sitting there than I did. Then I thought maybe it had less to do with putting on the creams and more about spending time together.

I was still thinking about this when Mrs. Szczygiel came into the bedroom to get something out of the closet. When she looked at me, she shrieked, "Mother! Come! Look! This child is burning up with fever!" Babcia came running in and slapped her hand to my forehead so hard that she nearly knocked my head against the wall. She looked perplexed to find that my head was cool, and when she turned around to tell Mrs. Szczygiel, she fixed her eyes on the dressing table. I looked over and realized I had forgotten to put the cover back on one of the jars. When Mrs. Szczygiel realized what Babcia had discovered, the two women burst out laughing. I was surprised that neither of them yelled at me for sitting at the table.

But the next day, a woman who lived on the same floor as ours in the building across the street saw

Mrs. Szczygiel at the market and asked about the young girl she'd seen through the bedroom window. When Mrs. Szczygiel came home, she was very upset with me. "Luncia, what's the matter with you?" she began. I knew I was in deep trouble. "I had to make up a story on the spot about my niece coming to visit," she went on. "And I'm sure the woman thought I was lying and she's going to report me, and then we'll all be finished!"

"I'm really sorry," I said, but she had already stormed away.

Babcia gave me a pitiful look. I was scared that Mrs. Szczygiel was so angry that she'd take me by my arm right down the stairs and leave me in the street. But she didn't. "Look," she said, coming back into the room. "Just please, please remember that you must stay on the couch. I know it's hard for a girl your age to sit still, but it's what you have to do for yourself and all of us." From then on, I obeyed.

From where I sat, I was barely able to see the clock on the far side of the bed, which I suppose was good because otherwise I'm sure it would have driven me mad, watching the hours pass so slowly. But I started to figure out about what time Mr. Szczygiel and the girls would get home based on how dark it was outside and how the shadows moved across the walls and furniture. Even through the thick bedroom door I could hear Jockey barking when he heard Mr. Szczygiel's key in the door.

Have I not mentioned Jockey? Jockey was Mrs. Szczygiel's little Chihuahua, and she'd fuss over him nonstop. You'd think he was her infant! She showed him more affection than she did her girls, constantly hugging and kissing him and letting him sit on her lap—even at the dinner table, from what Jasia told me—completely ignoring Mr. Szczygiel's protests. Sometimes I wished I were Jockey so Mrs. Szczygiel would treat me that way. I think her daughters felt somewhat the same.

Even though it felt like years, Christmas came only a few weeks from the time I got there. Hela couldn't stop talking about how her boyfriend, Marek, was coming over on Christmas. You would have thought she expected him to propose to her right at the table the way she went on about it! Jasia and Marysia had little patience for her antics, because every time Hela started to mention it, one of them would cut in and say, "Oh, Hela! Enough already!"

One thing that they all did talk about together was

the Christmas tree. I couldn't image what it was like having a real tree in the house. They talked about how good it would smell and how they planned to decorate it. Mrs. Szczygiel and Babcia's favorite topic of discussion was how they were going to prepare the meat for dinner, since it wasn't often that they had the chance to do so anymore.

On Christmas Eve, the three girls were going crazy trying to figure out what dresses to wear, while Mrs. Szczygiel baked cookies that were hung on the tree for decoration. Babcia made more decorations out of colorful paper, and when Mr. Szczygiel came home with the tree, she ran to get a little rug out of the closet and put it on the floor for the tree to stand on. The rug was so pretty—it was red and white with gold stitching around the edges. It reminded me of the silky little place mat my mother would put under our menorah, except ours was blue and white with silver trim.

It was nice to have the house so busy and joyful, but it made me a little sad because it reminded me of Hanukkah. My mother would stand over the stove all afternoon, frying potato latkes in oil, and the house would smell so good! We'd set up the menorah by the window, and when it got dark, Tatu would let me pick out the colors of the candles. I'd always choose blue for the *shammes*, which had its own spot on the top of the menorah and was used to light the rest of the candles.

The tree was put in the bedroom because there was no room in the living room. I was happy that I'd have something new to look at during the day, and the tree *did* smell wonderful. It smelled like outside, and because I hadn't been outside for more than a month, I was glad to be reminded of what it was like.

On Christmas Eve, Jasia disappeared into the closet and came out holding a green box. Marysia removed its cover and started taking out lovely glass ornaments while Mr. Szczygiel put the tree in its place in the corner. Mrs. Szczygiel came over and attached a few tiny metal candlesticks with colorful candles in them. They were so beautiful, but again I was reminded of Hanukkah and had to choke back my tears. I missed my mother and Tatu so much at that moment that I felt like the loneliest person in the world. Mrs. Szczygiel saw that I was upset and somehow she must have known what I was feeling because she went into the kitchen and came back with a book of matches and lit a few candles to cheer me up. It gave me such a warm feeling inside that it did make me smile.

Then something happened that took me by complete surprise. Mrs. Szczygiel walked over to Mr. Szczygiel and the two of them had a conversation in whispers. Then they came over and Mr. Szczygiel said, "We can't stand the thought of you being all alone in the room for Christmas. So come and sit in the kitchen, and we'll figure out a way to hide you so that you can be with us." Then he told me to sit on the floor by the wall all the way in the back. He left and came back carrying a drying rack with damp clothes hanging on it and placed it in front of me so I'd be completely hidden.

Suddenly, the doorbell rang. The guests had arrived! Everyone began talking and laughing, and then there was silverware clanking against plates. And the food! The smell of the food was so delicious it was almost more painful being in the kitchen than in the bedroom alone. I started to play a game with myself, trying to guess what it all was — meat with gravy, potatoes, dumplings. I wanted so much to eat it. Then I heard Hela say she needed to get something in the kitchen, and the next thing I knew I saw her arm sticking through the clothing on the rack. In her hand was a large hunk of bread with butter and soaked in gravy, and one of the cookies from the tree. "Here," she whispered. "Merry Christmas, Luncia!" I was very grateful.

Christmas came with the same amount of buzzing in the house as the evening before, except that Hela was even more frustrated getting dressed because her boyfriend, Marek, was coming. I was told to stay in my usual spot on the couch, and so I got to watch her put a dress on, look in the mirror, sigh, take it off, and put on another. This went on for three or four dresses until she had on her navy blue one and the doorbell rang. The choice was made for her! She quickly put on some more lipstick and opened the bedroom door just wide enough to slip out, so no one would see me sitting there.

There was conversation and laughter, and everyone sounded as if they were having a great time. Every so often I heard Hela's high-pitched laugh following Marek's deep voice. I imagined she laughed because Marek said something she thought was funny, or at least she tried to pretend she thought it was funny. But later in the evening I heard Marek's voice closer to the bedroom calling out, "Marysia?" And then I heard and saw the doorknob turn. I knew I was supposed to hide under the bed, but somehow I dove the wrong way and slid underneath the tree. Luckily, it was getting dark outside and the room was filled with long, gray shadows because Marek mistook me for Marysia and thought she was playing a joke on him. I heard Mrs. Szczygiel rush in. With her quick wit she said, "Don't be such a stubborn girl, Marysia, coming in here to pout after our silly little argument, when you should be in the living room with the guests." Then she closed the bedroom door. Marysia had gone out to the bathroom, and Mrs. Szczygiel rushed to find her to tell her to go back into the living room pouting, acting as if she were angry. My heart was pounding. I pulled my legs underneath me, deciding to stay under the tree for a few more minutes in case someone else opened the door. After a while, no one did, so I crawled over to the couch and, completely exhausted, put my head down and went to sleep.

After that close call, every day that I was in the apartment I was afraid of being discovered. Before there was only boredom and sadness, and now there was anxiety, too.

And this made it worse. One day when everyone was at work and Babcia was out visiting a sick friend, Mrs. Szczygiel had to go out for a while but couldn't find her keys. "Luncia, you have to do me a favor," she said. "I have no idea where my keys are, and I need to go out. When you hear me knock like this on the door you'll know it's me, so let me in." She knocked on the door in a pattern for me to hear. "Got it?" she said.

"Yes," I said. "I'll open it only for you."

A few hours later, I thought I heard her special knock, but when I opened the door there was a man in a uniform standing there! I thought he was a Nazi, so I turned and ran.

Later, I learned that he was the mailman, because a neighbor said he was trying to deliver the mail and a crazy little girl opened the door and ran away. Mrs. Szczygiel had to tell the story about me being her niece again.

"How could you have made such a mistake?" she scolded me. I felt awful and had nothing to say other than that I was sorry again.

A few weeks later, a well-known psychic came to Lvov to visit her relatives. Mrs. Szczygiel told Babcia and me that she had made an appointment to see her. I didn't know what a psychic was, so this matter didn't concern me. Babcia seemed very agitated and implored her daughter not to go. "After all" said Babcia "this woman might know that you have a Jewish child at home and report you to the German police."

Not taking her mother's advice, Mrs. Szczygiel decided to keep her date with the psychic. The next day, after she left the house, Babcia was very nervous. She even came to see me at my usual place: the dark corner of the bedroom, and explained what a psychic was, and what horrible things could happen. Hearing all this from Babcia, who usually was a calm person, frightened me, too. We both waited impatiently for Mrs. Szczygiel's return. After what seemed like ages, the front door opened, revealing her beaming face.

"Tell us quickly what happened!" said Babcia excitedly.

After sitting down and taking a sip of water from the glass that Babcia put in front of her, Mrs. Szczygiel, looking at both of us with a serious expression on her face, began describing in detail what had happened that morning. "I was ushered into a room that had heavy, crimson-colored draperies on the windows.

Between the two windows of the room stood a little table covered wth a table cloth which matched the draperies. A middle-aged woman with a kindly face sat behind the table. She motioned to me to sit down in a chair opposite hers. After a few moments, she started telling me about what my hobbies are. After a few minutes, with a serious expression on her face, she said to me, 'You have a little Jewish girl in your house. Keep her. Save her life. She will grow up to be an important person.'"

Babcia and Mrs. Szczygiel hugged in their excitement to get such good news. Even I got a kiss from the usually reserved ladies. I believe this psychic was one of the reasons the Szczygiels kept me for as long as they did.

One evening, Mr. Szczygiel was coming home from work when he ran into the landlord on his way upstairs. The landlord told him that he wanted to paint the apartment and would begin the following day. Of course, there was no way I could stay there with the painters, so the Szczygiels had to figure out what to do with me. Again I was terrified that I'd be put out on the street, but the next morning when I woke up Mr. Szczygiel told me he'd bring me down to the basement in the morning. I'd stay there during the day, and he would come get me in the evening after the painters left. The question was how to get me down there without anyone seeing.

"Here, get in here," Mr. Szczygiel finally said as he held open a burlap sack. "I'll cover your head with some pieces of wood and carry you to the basement." I got inside and the burlap made my nose itch. "Hold on to the wood at the ends so you don't get hit in the head," he said.

"But what if I get a splinter?" I asked.

"Would you rather get a splinter, which I can remove from your finger, or a concussion?" he asked.

I tried to hold the wood carefully, and then he threw the sack with me inside over his shoulder and walked down the stairs. I felt like garbage getting taken out to the curb. When we got to the basement, he had me sit on a little stool in the family's storage cubicle and then promised he'd come back to get me at the end of the day.

For a few minutes after he left it was completely silent. Then something rustled in the corner, making me jump up off my seat. The light was dim and so I couldn't make out what it was at first, and then I saw it. It was a rat! I'd never seen a live rat before, and its beady eyes were staring right at me. As frightened as I was, I was also relieved that it wasn't a person.

Then I started to notice that the rat had friends. All day they scuttled around, popping in and out of their holes. After I got over being afraid, it was actually entertaining to watch them.

Just as Mr. Szczygiel promised, he came to pick me up and bring me back upstairs when he came home from work. But there was bad news: The painters hadn't finished and would have to come back the next day. The next morning Mr. Szczygiel carried me back down to the basement in the burlap sack, and I watched the rats. When he came for me in the evening, he told me that I'd have to spend one more day down there because the painters still weren't finished. By this time I had started to actually miss sitting on the burgundy loveseat. Luckily, after the third day, the job was finished and that was the end of my time in the basement.

After I had been in hiding for about three months, Mrs. Szczygiel came home from shopping with news that changed how I looked at my life. My parents were still alive! She told me that she'd run into Mrs. Oyak, who had worked with my parents in their candy shop. Apparently, Tatu had arranged for Mr. Oyak to hide my mother at their house, and Mrs. Oyak often saw Tatu, who was still working outside the ghetto.

I realized that up until the moment Mrs. Szczygiel told me this, I had completely lost hope that my life would ever be the same again. But now there was a glimmer that maybe somehow, someday, everything could be good again.

That evening, Mrs. Szczygiel went to see the Oyaks and my mother. My mother had smuggled some of my best clothes out of the ghetto with her and gave them to Mrs. Szczygiel to bring to me. Seeing my good clothes made me want to be free again, to go outside and twirl in the street in my favorite outfit — my white spring coat and matching hat with big royal blue checks. But Mrs. Szczygiel said she'd have to go into the surrounding farm villages and trade the clothes for food. She must have seen the light in my eyes fade when she told me this, because then she said, "Why don't you go ahead and put it on, Luncia? I would love to see how pretty you must look in it."

"Oh, thank you," I said. "I'd like that very much."

I tried on my coat and hat one more time. Mrs. Szczygiel took the stool from the dressing table and brought it to the other side of the room away from the window. She helped me up onto it so I could see my whole self in the mirror. I must admit that I did look very pretty, and so I decided to pretend I was going for a walk.

Somehow, from that moment on, I felt things begin to change. Winter was coming to an end, and I could hear the sound of birds chirping outside. Now that it was getting warmer, Mrs. Szczygiel kept the window open all the time so I could get some fresh air. I breathed in the delicious scents from the street and the sweet smell of new leaves and grass growing. My favorite thing was listening to the children play. As they called to one another, I started to learn their names and pretend I was playing, too—games like jump rope and hopscotch and tag.

Knowing my parents were alive, I started reliving all the happy memories from my past. I would talk to myself and tell myself stories—real stories, not the fairy tales I'd been recalling all those months. Because I was used to whispering to others in the apartment, I started to whisper to myself, too. One day Mrs. Szczygiel came in and heard me and said, "You're talking to yourself, girl!" I didn't even realize it. From then on, I was very careful to speak to myself only in my thoughts.

Then came more good news: The Oyaks were now hiding Tatu! Mrs. Oyak had gone to visit Tatu at work to bring him some food and regards from my mother, and he told her that there were rumors that all the Jews who worked where he did would be shot within a few days. Mrs. Oyak told him to take off his armband and follow her home.

But then one day something terrifying happened. It was a few weeks later, and Marysia was sick and stayed home from work. She spent the day in the bedroom with me, sleeping for most of the day, but in the late afternoon her coworker, Alex, came to see her. No one had given me any warning, so when I saw and heard the doorknob turn, I barely had time to get under the bed. Jockey was in the room with us, too, and so he started barking and pawing at me because he thought I was playing a game. Alex kept looking under the bed to see what was going on, and

Marysia kept trying to get him to look out the window by asking him what the weather was like. The next moment, Mrs. Szczygiel came in and Jockey ran out.

After this happened, the girls realized that they wouldn't be so lucky forever, that eventually they might all get caught and killed, and so they begged their parents to make me leave.

In some ways I could understand their fear, but it made me feel so unwanted and awful. I heard Mr. Szczygiel say to Babcia that it wasn't fair for them to sacrifice six lives for one. But what could they do with me? Babcia and Mrs. Szczygiel came up with an idea—they would hide me from the rest of the family.

There was an old wooden trunk that sat underneath the kitchen window. When Mr. Szczygiel and the girls left for work, Babcia and Mrs. Szczygiel started working on my new hiding place. They found Mr. Szczygiel's toolbox and a handsaw and cut a hole in the side of the trunk so I could breathe. They put a blanket on the bottom. At five-thirty, just before everyone came home from work, Babcia helped me into the trunk. "Here," she said. "Hold on to my hand so you don't fall over. Whatever position you choose now is how you'll be for the rest of the night, so make sure it's at least a little bit comfortable."

As small and skinny as I was, the trunk was short and I had to curl up. Just as I heard the family's footsteps in the hall, Mrs. Szczygiel passed a wet rag through the hole. "There's oxygen in water, and it will help you breathe better if you keep it against your face," she said. I had no idea what oxygen was, but I thought I should listen because she seemed to know what she was talking about.

After a few hours my legs went numb. Jockey stuck his face in the little opening and tried to lick me and then tried to paw at me until Mrs. Szczygiel came over and scooped him up onto her lap. I heard everyone having dinner and getting ready for bed, but I was much too uncomfortable to sleep. I couldn't even turn over on my side because there wasn't any room. Then a pang of anxiety struck me and I felt claustrophobia for the first time in my life. I imagined I was in my own coffin, and I couldn't wipe the thought from my mind. My racing thoughts kept me up most of the night until finally it was morning and I was allowed out. Babcia opened the trunk and took my hand to help me up. It took me a few minutes to straighten my legs, and then Babcia led me to the burgundy couch, where I sat, had some food, and then was helped back into the trunk.

This went on for three weeks. Early one morning before work, Marysia leaned on the trunk while looking out the window and heard me move inside. She opened the lid of the trunk — and there I was. She ran to her family, telling everyone what she saw, and they came running in to make sure she wasn't seeing things. They all started to laugh and said that their mother and grandmother had played a clever trick on them. All I could think was, "Now I will have to die."

The next morning, Mrs. Szczygiel told me that she'd have to take me to the Oyaks'. When she first said this, I was thrilled because I'd finally be with my parents. But then I had a second thought. What if she was lying and she planned to abandon me in the street? After all, she could have asked the Oyaks to take me the moment she found out they were hiding my parents. I had assumed that there was no room at the Oyaks', or she would have, especially when her family demanded that I leave. I couldn't ask her if this was what she planned to do. All I could do was think about what Mother and Tatu said—that I had to believe I was going to survive.

After weeks in the trunk, I had forgotten how to walk properly. And after eight months in hiding, being allowed only to whisper, I'd forgotten how to speak in an audible voice. When I opened my mouth to speak, I sounded like a rooster crowing. There was no way I could leave the apartment until I could reverse these two things, or else someone might suspect something strange about me.

Babcia began to teach me how to walk and speak properly again. She'd lead me by my arm, reminding me to bend my knees, as we walked back and forth in the bedroom away from the window. It was much harder than you'd expect.

"I can't keep going, Babcia," I'd say to her after a short time. "I'm tired."

"You have to keep going if you're going to get strong enough to go outside," she said. "How would it look if a young girl like you didn't have a spring in every step she took? From me, people would expect someone bumbling along on the sidewalk. But not from you!"

After my walking lesson, she would sit me on the couch and, so no one would hear me, wrap my face in a thick scarf and make me repeat words out loud. It was hard for me not to laugh when we did this, because all my words would come out sounding like I was underwater, and I'd start to giggle in the scarf and then we'd have to start all over again! We practiced for a few days until she decided I'd made enough progress.

Finally, the day came for me to leave. I had such mixed emotions — I was elated at the thought of seeing my parents again, but at the same time I didn't believe that it was going to happen. I still wasn't sure if Mrs. Szczygiel was going to leave me in the street. She tried to make me look as presentable as possible, but I'd grown in the eight months I was in hiding and the only decent dress I had was short on me. My shoes were so tight that I begged Mrs. Szczygiel to let me leave them unlaced, but she said it was too risky, and so I squeezed my feet inside and tied the laces.

After I kissed Babcia, Mr. Szczygiel, and the girls good-bye, Mrs. Szczygiel and I walked down the stairs and into the street. Blinded by the bright sunshine, I closed my eyes and let the warmth of the sun envelop my entire body. Slowly, opening one eye at a time, my gaze fell on a tree across the street. It was so green, and its beautifully shaped leaves gently fluttered in the summer breeze. I looked up and saw a perfectly blue sky, dotted by small white clouds that looked like feathers spilling out of a torn pillow. Pink, red, and purple flowers were blooming in the window box of a blue house. All the colors around me were intensely vibrant, and it seemed as if I were looking at everything for the very first time. Then Mrs. Szczygiel's voice brought me back to reality. "We must hurry so we won't miss the bus," she said, taking my hand, and in that instant I knew that my fears of her abandoning me were unfounded.

We walked down the streets, past shops and carts and busy people rushing places, and got to the bus just in time. It was crowded, but we found two seats together. I was very involved with looking out the window, but after what seemed like only a few minutes Mrs. Szczygiel whispered to me that we must get off at the next stop. "Are we there already?" I asked.

"No, but I think someone is looking at you," she mumbled in my ear with a worried expression on her face.

We got off the bus and began walking, and ahead of us I saw a park and hoped that we'd walk through it. We did. The grass was thick, and I imagined that if I were to lie down on it it would feel cool against my arms and legs. There were wildflowers—lots of them. Even the weeds were lovely. The trees stood tall and straight and looked majestic against the sky. It seemed as if they couldn't be afraid of anything. At that moment, I wished I were a tree.

Finally, we came to Zielona Street, where the Oyaks lived. It was hard to believe I was about to see my parents for the first time in eight months. I wondered if they would look different to me. I wondered if they'd say I had changed. But again I was afraid. Would the Oyaks let me stay? What would happen if they didn't?

Mrs. Szczygiel rang the doorbell. The door opened and I looked straight up at the four overjoyed faces in the entrance, the Oyaks on one side and my parents on the other. Then eight arms reached out and pulled me close, nearly suffocating me with affection.

"Oh, Luncia, you've gotten so big!" my mother said. "I can't believe I'm actually looking at you!" Tatu put his hands on my shoulders and said, "My baby, my baby girl," and kept on pulling me close to kiss me, pushing me away to look at me, then pulling me close again for more kisses.

"I never thought I'd see you again," I said to them both, and we all embraced. "It's been so hard without you." I was trying to tell them about how wonderful the walk was to the Oyaks' apartment but kept getting interrupted with more kisses and hugs. Finally, to no one in particular, I blurted out: "The world is so beautiful! I want so much to live!"

For a moment, I thought I'd said something wrong because my parents started to cry. The Oyaks and Mrs. Szczygiel cried, too. Then, in a very emotional voice, Mr. Oyak said, "Let her stay. It's the same death whether I am hiding one, two, or three people."

Part III: A New Life

Being reunited with my parents in hiding was a huge relief and gave me hope for the future, but our daily lives were still very hard. Food was just as scarce at the Oyaks' as it had been at the Szczygiels', though now when I was hungry I had my mother to complain to, which made me feel better, although I'm sure it annoyed her no end. After all, she was hungry as well, and it must have been difficult for her to be patient with me, which she somehow always managed to be.

The Oyaks' apartment was bigger than the Szczygiels', with a large kitchen, a living and dining room, a bedroom, a common room, and a bathroom that had a huge porthole above the tub. Strangely, the porthole wasn't a window, and Tatu said that this was his hiding place. When a visitor came to the apartment, he'd curl himself up inside the hole and Mrs. Oyak would hang a washtub over the opening. It was customary in European homes to have a wall with a door dividing the toilet and the sink from the tub area, and so people who used the toilet usually didn't even go near the tub.

At first I couldn't imagine Tatu scrunching up small enough to fit inside the hole. It barely looked big enough for me. "There's no way you can fit inside that," I said to him. "It's too small! Show me!"

"Okay," he said. "I wish I had something to bet you, because if I did you would lose!"

If we hadn't been in hiding, Tatu probably wouldn't have gone to all the trouble of getting in and out, but he would do anything to make me smile a little. He stood on the rim of the tub and hoisted himself up, then pulled his legs into his chest and tucked his head over his knees, using his hands to pull down on his neck to make himself as small as possible. He looked like what I imagined a snail would if I could see it inside its shell. "See," he said. "I told you I could do it!"

The Oyaks slept in the bedroom, and my parents and I slept in the common room. They shared a cot in the corner and I slept on the table, which sounds awful but was more comfortable than you'd think. My mother gathered some of Mrs. Oyak's rags, washed them, and stuffed them inside pillowcases she made from an old pair of curtains. Even though it was a hard surface rather than the soft bed I had shared with Babcia and Marysia at the Szczygiels', at least it was my own place to sleep! No one complained if I moved around during the night, and it was much nicer and more comforting to listen to the sound of my parents' steady breathing than to Babcia's hiccupping snores.

I was lucky to have a mother so skilled with a needle and thread, because I had only one pair of socks at that point and was constantly putting holes in them. My mother had an old pair of stockings and reinforced the soles of my socks with them, but that did little to keep my toes from poking through. My feet had grown since the socks were new, bright white, and pretty against my shiny black patent leather shoes. "Just look at them now," I said to her. "They're so dirty and gray, it's depressing!"

"You're right," she said. "We need to do something about them. It's no way for a pretty young girl to walk around, even if you're not leaving the house. Maybe I can borrow some ink from Mrs. Oyak and dye them for you. It's not a perfect solution, but at least they won't look dirty anymore." My mother was able to borrow some navy dye and they did look better. My shoes were the last of my belongings we gave to the Oyaks to sell for food, but I wasn't sorry to have to give them up because they were tight, and I couldn't wear them in the house, anyway, because the downstairs neighbors might hear my footsteps.

Having spent most of my days during the eight months at the Szczygiels' in complete silence, I felt lucky to have my parents around to talk to. We'd quietly share stories of our lives before we were in hiding, and we'd try our best to collectively remember all the details we feared we'd forget. We talked about our apartment and where everything was kept and what our favorite things were that we'd had to leave behind. We talked about afternoons at Sarotina and the new kinds of candy Tatu would try to make, and how excited everyone in the neighborhood was the summer we bought the colorful ice-cream machine for the store's window.

"I miss the things I'd bring out from the china cabinet each year for us to use on special occasions," my mother said. "Like the plate we used for your birthday cake, Luncia—do you remember the one, with blue and white stripes? It was made by your great-aunt when you were born. And then there was the tablecloth with the edging embroidered by my grandmother that we used only on holidays. It was comforting to see those things year after year, even if they were just things."

"I remember the dish," I said. "When I was really little I thought the stripes were part of the cake's icing, and I remember sticking my finger on them and finding out that they weren't something I could eat!"

"Speaking of eating," Tatu said, "I miss tasting the first piece of candy in the morning. Even though I always had my coffee before I went to the store, I didn't feel as if I was really awake until that sweet hit my lips. I'd say to myself as I ate it, 'May life always be as sweet as this,' and then pop it in my mouth. It was how I started my day. Now the days just run together without any beginning or end."

There was one happy thing from my old life that was rekindled at the Oyaks': getting to watch my father play chess. Tatu was teaching Mr. Oyak how to play, and the two men would sit for hours at a time. Mr. Oyak had a hard time winning against Tatu. When he found out that I knew how to play, too, Mr. Oyak decided to enlist me, thinking it would be better to play against someone at the same level. I much preferred watching chess to playing it, but every Sunday Mr. Oyak would challenge me to a tournament and

I'd have no choice but to oblige. I'd hear those words I dreaded. "Okay, Luncia," Mr. Oyak would say. "How about giving this old man a little brain challenge?" I'd groan quietly to myself and my mother would shoot me a look of disapproval.

Before long, I was able to beat him regularly, and he'd grow frustrated and keep me at the table for hours. One afternoon, my mother kicked me under the table and whispered that I should start letting him win once in a while, which I tried to do, but it was hard to figure out how to play poorly after I'd learned to play so well.

While the Oyaks went out during the day, my parents had to be extra careful to not make any noise in the apartment, not even to whisper to each other. Mrs. Oyak would come and go a lot, as she had family in the surrounding villages to visit, and so we'd sit still and busy ourselves with what we could find to occupy our time. Tatu would read the newspaper and my mother would sew, and I'd either help her or doodle with a pencil on scraps of paper. Sometimes I missed having Jockey around to watch. He wasn't my dog, and he could be annoying when he whined for food or barked at the door, but I became sort of attached to him because I could always rely on his antics to entertain me.

Then one afternoon Mrs. Oyak came home with a white rabbit! One of her relatives had given it to her, and she decided to keep it in a crate in the bathroom next to the tub. Its eyes were like little black buttons and its fur was as soft as velvet, and I spent as much time as I could stroking it and pretending it was my pet.

Winter had arrived, and so there was even less to eat than during the warmer months. Mrs. Szczygiel came to visit often, and she would bring scraps of food in a paper bag for the rabbit. I wondered why the rabbit got extra food and we didn't, and apparently my mother wondered the same thing because one afternoon she asked Mrs. Szczygiel if we could share some of what she brought for the rabbit. Even though I was glad my mother asked — sometimes I was so hungry that I'd nearly faint if I stood up too quickly — I was also embarrassed. It was hard to think of us as so desperate that we were asking to share food with a rabbit. But from then on, Mrs. Szczygiel came with a separate bag for us filled with pieces of potato and heels of bread.

Soon it was Christmas again. The Oyaks weren't particularly religious, and so they just celebrated the holiday with a bit of extra food. The day before, Mrs. Oyak left the house with the rabbit's crate in her arms and came home carrying a big package. She didn't seem to have the rabbit with her. Soon the wonderful smell of meat cooking filled the kitchen, and I was overcome with hunger and began to salivate. Then I was instantly struck by the terrible realization that I was smelling the little white rabbit boiling in the pot on the stove. I ran over to my mother and buried my head in her chest, and Mrs. Oyak said, "But, Luncia, rabbit stew is delicious! Don't you want to try some?" She came over with a little piece of meat on a fork, which I refused to taste or even look at.

Just then, Mr. Oyak came in and told Mrs. Oyak that his mother asked to spend the night at their house on Christmas Eve with her German friend. "I can't say no," he told her. "How strange would that look? If I say no she'll definitely suspect that something is going on. We have no choice. We need to figure something out."

"You're right," Mrs. Oyak said. "But we need to figure it out quickly!"

The adults decided that Tatu should go to his usual

hiding place in the porthole. Mr. Oyak would tell his mother and her guest that the bathtub was out of order and they could only use the toilet and the sink on the other side of the door. The part of the bathroom where the tub was would be locked.

Finding a hiding place for mother and me wasn't as easy. My mother's hiding place had been the bottom half of the bookcase in the bedroom, and we didn't think I could fit in there as well. But with no other option, we had to make it work. My mother lined the bottom of the bookcase with some of the rags she'd washed to make the pillows, which I thought she did so we'd be more comfortable, and then she climbed inside. I climbed in after her, scrunching up tight and sitting between her legs. "Luncia," she said, "feel for a nail sticking out at the top of the inside of the cabinet door. Do you feel it?"

"I think so," I said. "I can barely reach it, though."

"Well," she continued, "you're going to have to grab onto it to shut the door. So stretch!"

Apparently, Mr. Oyak had hammered a nail there so my mother could close herself inside quickly. I did as she told me, and we sat together in the darkness. I was scared and anxious, mostly because it was stressful to have to think of a plan so quickly. But I started calming down once my mother began to stroke my hair and as the warmth of her body enveloped me.

A moment later, the doorbell rang. I heard what I imagined was Tatu's soft, fast footsteps head toward the bathroom, which reminded me that, before getting into the bookcase in the midst of all the chaos, I hadn't had a chance to go. Before long I heard glasses clinking and people singing Christmas carols, and to take my mind off having to use the toilet I tried pretending that I was at the party, too, in a pretty dress, running around and playing with the other children. But it was no use. "Mother," I whispered, "I'm sorry, but I have to go to the bathroom. What am I going to do?"

"Why do you think I put all these rags in here?" she asked. "Do what you have to do."

As uncomfortable as it was, I had no choice, and then my mother pushed the soiled rags into the far corner of the shelf with her foot and told me to try to go to sleep. Eventually, I did.

I woke up the next morning to the smell of freshly brewed coffee and remembered dreaming that I was sleeping in my own comfortable bed in our old apartment, but I didn't know why I couldn't stretch out my legs. Then I felt a pang of anxiety thinking about the last time I'd woken up in such a tight space, feeling sore with leg cramps. It was when Mrs. Szczygiel and her mother had hidden me from the rest of the family in the old wooden trunk in the kitchen under the window. I shuddered at the thought, wondering how I ever survived that ordeal every day for three weeks.

After a while we heard Mr. Oyak's mother and her German friend leave, and within a few moments we heard a knock on the other side of the bookcase door. This was my mother's signal that it was safe for her to come out. I slowly unfolded myself as I climbed out, remembering from my time in the trunk at the Szczygiels' that if I got out too fast I'd get shooting pains in my legs. My mother got out slowly, too, and then got our paper bag from Mrs. Szczygiel from the kitchen. "Here," she said to me, "have something to eat. Food in your stomach will soothe you and you'll feel better in a minute or two."

She was right. I stood there chewing for a long time, because the bread had grown very stale, and suddenly felt tears streaming down my cheeks, though I managed to wipe them away quickly enough so that no one saw. I couldn't figure out why I was crying, and then it hit me: It had been more than a year since I'd been living this way, and there didn't seem to be an end in sight.

Several months later, Mrs. Oyak came home from visiting relatives and said she'd heard rumors that a deserter from the German army was hiding out in the neighborhood and the Gestapo were going to search for him. My father had his good hiding place in the porthole, but apparently bookcases and other types of cabinets were popular hiding places and didn't fool the Gestapo. So my mother decided that we'd be safest if we left the house early and stayed away until it was dark.

We left the apartment first thing the next morning, and after walking only a few short blocks we ran into an old acquaintance of my mother's, a Gentile woman. "Mrs. Gamzer," she said, "what are you doing here? I thought that all the Jews of Lvov had already been killed!" She almost shouted the last part of her sentence, and a group of children, sensing her excitement, began to surround us. My mother shot a fast, polite smile at the woman, took my hand, and led me down a side street until we came to a park. We'd brought one of the bags filled with heels of bread, and we sat down to have something to eat.

After sitting a while my mother said she had a surprise. "Luncia," she said, "look what I have!" She pulled a few coins out of her pocket.

"Where did you get those?" I asked.

"It's from a very little bit of savings your father and I have been keeping. He didn't want us to be out in the street without money. We can find a restaurant to sit down in and have some tea to get out of the cold."

"Oh, Mother," I said, "that sounds wonderful! Imagine—sitting down in a restaurant just like we used to!" Back then, of course, I could order just about anything I felt like eating, but that didn't matter. It was a chance for us to relive a little bit of our old life, even if it was just for a little while.

We ordered our tea, but after taking a few sips my mother grabbed my hand under the table, leaned over, and said in a worried voice, "I think some of those people are looking at us. Hurry up and finish, Luncia, because we need to go quickly without seeming suspicious. We'll try to pretend we're late for an appointment." I did as I was told and then quickly put my coat on. "Hurry up," my mother said loud enough so others could hear. "We're going to be late for your piano lesson."

We hurried out of the restaurant and walked down another street. The sun was setting and the air was growing colder, even though spring had arrived. We didn't have proper outer clothes, and so when the wind picked up it felt as if it was blowing right through us. I wanted so badly to go back to the Oyaks', but we had to stay out a little longer.

Suddenly, I thought about Tatu. "Mother," I said urgently, "I just thought of something. What if the Gestapo go into the apartment and discover Tatu's hiding place?"

"We just have to have hope, Luncia," she said. "It'll be dark soon and we'll be able to go back." Finally, after what seemed like several hours, darkness enveloped the city and my mother said it was time to leave the streets.

When we got back to the Oyaks', I ran to Tatu and gave him a huge hug. "Oh, Tatu," I blubbered. "I was so worried about you. I just started to think the worst!" It was the first time that we had been separated since I'd joined my parents in hiding, and it made me realize how blessed we were to be together all the time.

"They caught the deserter in the late afternoon," Mrs. Oyak said. "Thankfully, it was pretty quiet around here for most of the day." Somehow, we had all survived the threat of death yet again.

Summer passed without any sign of the war ending. Things were a little bit better for us and for the Oyaks during the summer, mostly because heating the apartment was too expensive in winter, and the warm weather brought occasional fresh fruit and vegetables. But when the apartment grew very hot, as it did on several evenings, the tension in the house grew as well. Mr. Oyak would come home from work and complain to Mrs. Oyak about spending the day in fear of having us discovered in their home. "You leave the house and go to work and can forget about them," she said. "I have to look at them all day, every day. I wouldn't mind being arrested, because sitting in jail I would mark days off a calendar and look forward to my freedom. But I'm afraid to die."

My parents felt very sorry that they'd put their friends in such a difficult position. They began to talk with Mr. and Mrs. Oyak about things so horrible I could barely listen. No one seemed to notice that I was in the room when my parents would suggest to the Oyaks ways of getting rid of us. "What if we swallow poison?" I overheard my mother saying to Mrs. Oyak.

"But then what will I do with your bodies?" she said. "Someone would know we were hiding Jews even after you were dead, and then we'd be killed, too."

A few days later it was the topic of discussion again. "We could go to our old apartment building and throw ourselves off the balcony," my mother suggested. "Then you wouldn't have to worry about what do to with us." It made me so upset to hear her speak of this that I started to cry. "No!" I screamed. "I won't let you throw me off a balcony!"

I think both women were surprised to learn that I'd been listening. "Oh, Luncia," my mother said, "I'm sorry. I shouldn't talk about such things — not in front of you, and not at all. It's just that your father and I feel so terrible about burdening the Oyaks for as long as we have."

But the discussions didn't stop. The Szczygiels would come to the Oyaks', and they and my parents would sit in the kitchen and try to come up with a solution after I'd gone to sleep — except I'd never actually be sleeping and would stay awake listening to them talk. "You could leave town and pretend to be homeless," one of them said. But then Mrs. Szczygiel's mother said, "I'd trust the parents if they were caught, but no one knows what the child would say if she were tortured by the Gestapo."

Everyone agreed. Nothing was said for a few minutes. They just sat and stared at one another. Then Mrs. Szczygiel came up with an idea that they all thought would work. "Well," she began, "I don't know if he'd agree to it, but one of my daughters has a boyfriend who is an undercover cop with the Polish police, and he owns a gun. I could confide in him that you're hiding a Jewish family and ask him to take them into the woods to shoot them."

My heart dropped to my feet when I heard this, and I could feel the blood drain from my face. How could they plan our deaths so casually? Normally, I would have screamed or run over to my mother, but I decided to convince myself that I was having a nightmare and go back to sleep.

But it wasn't a nightmare. This was really going to happen. The arrangements were made, and I heard Mrs. Oyak tell my mother that we were going to be killed the following day. The policeman would come for us at seven P.M.

When I woke up the next morning, it seemed for a moment like just another day. Then I realized that it was the day I was going to die, and it suddenly felt as if my arms, legs, and then the rest of my body were engulfed in flames. Throughout the afternoon no one spoke about the fact that it was to be the last day of our lives.

The sun went down, and chilly air penetrated the room we were sitting in. It was getting dark, and with every moment that passed I felt myself grow more and more anxious. Every time I heard footsteps on the staircase, my heart would drop. I started to shiver, not just because it was getting cold, but because I was terrified. I started to watch the clock on the wall. Five o'clock came and went. Then six o'clock. With rising hysteria, I climbed into my mother's lap and began pulling on her clothes and scratching her chest in a desperate effort to try to hide myself inside her body.

Then it was seven o'clock. I was afraid to breathe. I kept my eyes on the clock and watched the minute hand move forward. Seven-fifteen, seven-thirty. I strained to hear footsteps in the hallway, but it was very quiet. Our executioner didn't come.

The next day Mrs. Szczygiel came to visit. "He said he couldn't do it," she said of the man who was to come kill us. "He said he wasn't a murderer and he was sorry but he couldn't go through with what he said he would do." For a moment then, when it truly felt as if we would die after having narrowly escaped death so many times already, I felt a little bit of hope. Maybe the war would end soon and my parents and I would survive it.

Several months passed. We woke one morning in July 1944 to the sound of gunshots in the street. Mrs. Oyak ran to the window to take a look outside. "I think it's the Russian army!" she said. "Is it possible?"

Mr. Oyak joined her at the window. "Yes!" he said. "I think we're being liberated!"

It was hard to know what to do right away. We were all in shock and had such mixed emotions. One minute I was overcome with happiness, the next I was confused and a little scared, and then I felt completely overwhelmed. But everyone in the apartment hugged and kissed and cried, and outside you could see people standing on their balconies waving to the soldiers in the street.

It wasn't as if our situation changed instantly. It took a few days for Hitler's army to leave Lvov, and so we stayed inside just in case there was a counterattack.

Tatu was the bravest of the three of us to take a walk in the city. Coming back, he told us that he saw a German tank in the middle of town. Hearing cries for help, he peeked inside and saw a young German soldier. The man clutched his bleeding shoulder, and noticing my father, asked him for help. By that time a group of people gathered around the tank, shouting: "You are our enemy. How dare you ask us for help!"

Not paying attention to the mob, Tatu saw to it that an ambulance was called and didn't leave the scene until the young boy was in the safe hands of the ambulance attendants.

After three days, Mrs. Oyak said it was safe for us all to go out. I ran down the staircase as fast as I could, though my knees felt a bit wobbly because I wasn't used to running. When I pushed the front door open and stepped into the sunshine, I took a deep breath, and it felt as if I were breathing—really breathing—for the first time. "Look at the sunlight!" I exclaimed as my parents came to join me. "Isn't it wonderful!"

"Yes," my mother said. "It's more than wonderful. It's a miracle."

As we walked across the city to see if our old apartment building was still intact, I felt as if I were in a dream or watching myself in a movie, like I was experiencing things through the eyes of a person outside of me. We'd turn down a particular street and I wouldn't think I knew the name, but when I saw it written on the sign high above my head, I realized I'd known it all along.

But our joy was quickly shattered within the next few hours. Tatu had tried to find friends and neighbors while my mother and I went back to the apartment. When he came back several hours later he had awful news: No one had survived. We were the only ones left.

It wasn't only extreme sadness I felt. Strangely, I felt guilty to be alive. Why had my parents and I been spared when everyone else had died? No matter how hard I tried, I couldn't stop asking myself that question. It was something that I kept coming back to for a very, very long time.

Starting our lives over again was a struggle. We were poorer than we'd ever been. We found an apartment near the Oyaks. There were no jobs in the city, and many people were without homes or work. Mrs. Oyak gave Tatu some sugar and other ingredients to make candy, and he made some wonderful rum balls. My mother found a tray to put them on, and she took them out to sell in the street.

After buying some food and paying off debts to Mr. Oyak and our superintendent, my mother bought me a new pair of shoes. I had been walking around in a ratty pair of Mrs. Oyak's straw slippers. There was a lot less money for clothes, but my mother got some inexpensive fabric and sewed me a very simple but pretty dress. It wasn't as special as the ones I wore before the war, but I was happy to have something new and clean.

Slowly, little bits and pieces of our old life came back. Tatu found work here and there and still made candy to sell on the side. My parents met a woman who was a piano teacher. My mother explained what a good music student I'd been, and the woman agreed to test my ability. Afterward, she offered to give me free lessons and let me go to her house every day to practice for as long as I wanted. How wonderful it was to be playing music again! It was hard to talk or even think about my experiences in hiding, but when I sat down to play the piano it was as if all my feelings came out through my fingers as I pressed down on the keys.

My parents also found a tutor to help me catch up with school, someone they'd known for years, and she offered to teach me for free. Her name was Miss Levitska. During the war, she had risked her life working in the Polish underground army because she was a great Polish patriot. She came every day for a few hours, and I read and did arithmetic for her. It felt good to be continuing with my studies, but it wasn't nearly as much fun as going to school had been. I missed having girlfriends around to play and laugh with, as my social circle now consisted only of my parents and my teachers. It was lonely being the only young person in adult company all the time, and I wished I had a brother or sister so that I'd have someone close to my age to talk to.

Then something wonderful happened. One sunny afternoon, Mrs. Szczygiel came to our apartment with a surprise for me. It was a puppy! Apparently, Jockey had become father to a litter of six, and this was one of the females. They had named her Lala, which is Polish for dolly, because she was small and delicate-looking.

"Oh, Mother, isn't she lovely?" I said. "Just look at her!" She was mostly black but had caramel-colored hair on her throat. She was a Chihuahua.

Lala quickly became the center of attention in our household. She was a poor eater, which caused us all to worry constantly about her health. She would eat only when she was happy, and she was at her happiest when we came home after being out. So Tatu came up with an idea. "Here's what we're going to do," he said. "Tonight, let's put on our coats and say elaborate good-byes to Lala. Then we'll leave the apartment and wait in the hallway for about fifteen minutes. When we walk back in, Lala will be so happy that I bet she'll run to her dish and gobble up her food!"

He was right—it happened just as he said it would, and so this became a nightly routine. Of course, Lala's favorite food was meat. As poor as we were, my mother would somehow manage to buy little scraps from the butcher, but they would be only for the dog. I was never allowed to touch any of it! "You can eat something else," my mother would say. "This is for Lala."

One day my parents came home with a man. They found him wandering the streets, trying desperately to find a surviving relative. Even though he did not find anyone, he was overjoyed to meet my parents, who told him that they were Jewish. Mother asked him to come home with them, since he didn't seem to want to let go of my parents. To my eyes he seemed quite old, even though he told us that he was twenty-two years old. His name was Adam.

Survivors, when they met for the first time, always asked, "How did you survive?" After drinking hot tea, Adam, with trembling lips, clenching and unclenching his fists, began telling his story. "I was taken away from the apartment that I lived in together with my parents. They were taken some weeks later. Together with my neighbors and many people I didn't know, I was driven in a truck to a railroad station where we were all loaded into a freight train.

"The train was packed to capacity. It was a very warm summer day. Pressed by so many people, I thought that I would suffocate. Piece by piece, I began to remove my clothing until I had on only my underwear. People were trying to guess where we were being taken. Somebody said that most probably we were being taken to a killing center where the Nazis would murder us with gas. My mind started to work feverishly, thinking of ways to escape. It was very dark in the freight car except for a beam of light coming through a tiny window. I began edging closer to the window. It was very small, but I thought that in my emaciated state I could probably push my body through it.

"After some time the train began to slow down. I pushed my head through this little window, and the rest of my body followed. I found myself lying on the ground, with grass and weeds all around me. The train vanished from view. Even though my arms and legs were very sore, I was able to stand up. Looking around, I recognized that I was in the outskirts of a town I knew very well. One of my schoolmates, a Christian girl named Teresa, lived nearby.

"Since it was getting dark, there were hardly any people in the streets. Walking as quickly as I could, I headed straight to Teresa's house."

Adam took a few more sips of his tea. I was fascinated by his tale and could hardly wait for him to continue. Finally, he resumed speaking. "Teresa, hearing my frantic knocking on her door, opened it and let me into her apartment. She told me that, even though they were not Jewish, her parents were taken away and sent to Germany to work in a factory. I stayed hidden in her house until the day the Germans left."

My parents were very eager to meet this wonderful, brave Teresa and kept asking Adam, who had become a frequent visitor, to bring her to our house. Adam always came up with an excuse not to do so.

Just as I was starting to feel settled in our new life, enjoying my studies and piano and playing with Lala, everything changed again. The Russians announced that the city of Lvov was now going to be part of the Ukraine instead of Poland. If we wanted to remain Polish citizens, we'd have to move to Kraków. If we stayed in Lvov, we'd have to become Russian citizens. My parents knew that it would be easier for us to eventually leave Europe and emigrate to the United States or Palestine (present-day Israel) if we moved, so they began making arrangements to leave.

We didn't have a lot of time to prepare. Knowing that we could bring only the essentials with us, we packed two small suitcases and told the neighbors to help themselves to the rest of our possessions. No one in my immediate family had ever lived outside Lvov, and so it was hard for me to imagine what it would be like to live in another city. I was sad to leave the only home I'd ever known, but I was also excited to be going to a new place where we could make a fresh start. At least we were bringing Lala with us.

All my anxiety and excitement were met by disappointment when we got to the train station. There was an announcement on the loudspeaker: No more trains were leaving for Kraków. We were told that we should stay at the station because no one was sure when the next train would come. Everyone stood around with bags, wondering what to do. Families who lived nearby came with hot soup, so we had something to eat. But we were stuck in the station almost two whole days before it was announced that we would be taken by trucks to Kraków the next day.

As we were waiting in the station that night, we suddenly spotted Adam, the survivor we had befriended. He was coming toward us, and beside him walked a woman who was clearly a hunchback. Her body was so deformed that her head seemed to be growing out of her shoulders.

The tall, handsome Adam introduced us to Teresa, the woman who had saved him, and her kind eyes looked up at him with great love.

As if to answer the astounded expression on our faces, Adam, leaning over to kiss us good-bye, whispered that he would never, till the end of his life, leave Teresa.

After a bumpy ride that lasted several hours, we arrived in Kraków and were taken to a warehouse where there were other families just like us who'd arrived from cities all over Poland. Even though I was very tired from the trip, I buzzed with energy being in an unfamiliar, busy city.

Then my parents saw a familiar face. Mother took my hand and we walked over to a Jewish man they knew from Lvov. He was with a woman and a little girl who was about five years old. The man's wife hadn't survived the war, but shortly after the liberation he'd remarried. After talking for a while, the couple and my parents decided that they'd look for a place to live together once they were able to leave the warehouse. I looked at the girl, whose name I can't recall, but I remember she was petite and had dark brown eyes and brown hair and was very pretty. She was too young to be a close friend, and I wished she was a little older because she seemed very nice. Even with Lala's company, I still longed to have a best girlfriend to spend time with.

After a few days, we found a three-room apartment with a shared kitchen and bathroom that suited us all. I shared a room with my parents, but Tatu managed to hang a curtain from the wall to the side of the window frame, so I had my own private little corner. It was almost as good as my own bedroom and felt cozy.

Soon after we moved in, Tatu registered me in a special school for Jewish children ages six to seventeen who had survived the war. Many were very behind with their studies, just like me. On my first day, my mother dressed me in the finest clothes I had at the time, which were plain but still pretty.

"Do I look okay?" I asked my mother.

"You look gorgeous," she said, kissing me on the cheek.

"But I'm nervous," I said. "I haven't been to school in such a long time! What if the kids don't like me? What if I'm very far behind everyone else?"

"Would you rather not go?" she asked, giving me a little smile. "Of course I want to go!" I cried. As nervous as I was, I was also excited to finally have the chance to make friends my age.

We had two teachers, also survivors, who practically had to teach us one-on-one because we were all at different levels. It was hard to go from not being busy at all to being almost too busy. I'd forgotten what it was like! I'd get up at six o'clock every day and my mother would have breakfast waiting, and then I'd walk to the school, which was about twenty-five minutes from our apartment. The school day was long, from seven to four, and we went six days a week, Sunday through Friday. Plus, I had to go all summer without a break! But within a few months, I'd finally finished all the requirements for my elementary school education. All my hard work had paid off.

Because we hoped to leave Poland as soon as possible, my parents rented me a piano instead of buying one. I continued my lessons with a great teacher, Mr. Brett, who was very strict and made me practice for more hours than I ever had before. "My fingers hurt," I'd complain to him.

"Aren't some sore fingers worth a chance at supporting yourself someday with your talent?" he'd ask.

I had to agree with him, although I couldn't imagine being able to earn a living playing the piano. But Mr. Brett had such confidence in me that it made me have confidence in myself.

Our lives were good in Kraków. I continued with school and finally found a group of girls to spend time with, including a girl named Pearl who became a good friend. I continued studying piano and improved tremendously under Mr. Brett's instruction. Lala stuck by my side, following close behind whenever she could, and slept on my pillow at night. When it was cold outside, I'd carry her under my coat on my chest to keep her warm because she was so tiny she'd shiver. Tatu made candy that my mother sold to several stores. Food in the city was plentiful, and so we had as much to eat as we wanted, including fresh fruits and vegetables, things that we'd only occasionally had in Lvov. Every so often a package filled with clothing and food would arrive from our relatives in America. Even though the clothes weren't new, I loved wearing what had belonged to my cousins. The styles were so modern in comparison to what I had! I'd try everything on as quickly as I could, looking in the mirror to see what fit and what didn't. I knew that I'd eventually be making a life for myself somewhere far away, maybe wearing clothes just like the ones that came in the packages. Putting them on was like practicing to be the person I was to become.

Then, in what seemed like no time at all, even though nearly two years had passed since we moved to Kraków, word came that we were granted passage to America. We were so excited to finally be leaving Poland! It was our true home, but the suffering we'd endured there made us want to put it behind us as soon as possible.

Our first stop would be a displaced persons camp in Austria, and from there we would go to to Munich,

Germany, which was under the control of the American government. From Munich we hoped to eventually get on a boat bound for New York City, where our family lived.

The only problem was Lala. My parents insisted that she was too frail to make such a long journey. "But why, why can't she come?" I pleaded with my mother.

"You know that the journey to America will be hard," she said. "Do you want her to get sick and die? You have to try to be a grown-up about this, Luncia."

As depressed as I was about leaving my dog behind, I knew they were right. I didn't want to risk her life, and so I agreed to give her back to the Szczygiels because I was sure she'd be well cared for. The day my mother took her on the bus to the Szczygiels' I cried terribly, and for several days afterward as well.

Just as when we had left Lvov, there wasn't much time for us to prepare to leave Kraków. We gathered only our basic necessities and told our neighbors to help themselves to everything we couldn't bring. I'd grown attached to my life in Kraków because I had settled into a routine for the first time since the war began.

And so in some ways I was sorry to have to leave, even though I knew in my heart that I didn't really want to stay.

Getting on the train for Austria was a lot easier than when we came to Kraków. It was a long train ride, though, and again we traveled with a large group of other refugees hoping to get to America. Because we could take only what we could carry, I didn't have anything to occupy me on the train except the scenery out the window, which was beautiful. After several hours, the train began to make its way through the Alps, and I saw rolling green hills and deep valleys and navy blue lakes. I'd never seen anything like it.

We finally arrived at the displaced persons camp in the small town of Steyr in Austria. Almost immediately, my eye caught another girl's and I knew she and I would become instant friends. Her name was Halina, and she had lovely blonde, straight hair that she wore down and loose. Within a few hours we were walking arm in arm through the picturesque town, seeing the sights and enjoying all the gardens in front of the neat little houses. She told me that her mother was a professor at the University of Kraków and her father had been separated from the rest of the family during the war. They suspected he'd been killed, although they didn't know when or where. "You're lucky you have both your parents," she said. I didn't know what to say that wouldn't make her feel bad, and so I just shook my head.

But then the week after we arrived, Halina and her mother received wonderful news. She came running over to me one morning saying, "Luncia! Luncia! My father! We just heard he's alive and living in London!" Apparently, he'd been looking for them for more than a year. "Now we're going to go there to meet him instead of going to America!" It was wonderful to witness a close friend be so incredibly happy. It gave me hope that even during terrible times, good things sometimes happen.

We stayed at the displaced persons camp for about six weeks before we could leave for Munich. It was very difficult to say good-bye to Halina, the first real best friend I'd had in many years. We swore to each other that we'd keep in touch no matter what, and we hugged and kissed until it was time for my family and me to leave.

Again my parents and I were on a train with other refugees. The trip to Munich wasn't nearly as pleasant as our trip to Austria. It was dark and gloomy when we arrived, and Munich wasn't nearly as charming as Steyr. I suddenly felt very depressed, longing for an end to our constant moving from one place to another. Along with other displaced persons, we were taken to a building that had formerly housed soldiers. There was one room with a concrete floor and about thirty beds. It looked like a prison.

My mother and I stayed behind while Tatu ventured into the city to find us a place to live. There, he met other displaced persons who had been living in Munich for a while and who already had apartments. He managed to find a room for us to rent in a large apartment owned by a man named Mr. Joseph Gelbart.

When Tatu came back and told my mother and me that we could leave right away, we couldn't have been happier. The thought of spending the night in the barracks was depressing. We quickly gathered our things and left.

The room we rented was already furnished with a sleeper sofa, a cot for me, and a table and chairs. "Well, there's at least enough room for an upright piano on that wall," my mother said to me, pointing to a corner of the room.

"I guess so," I said, trying to sound a little excited. I already had the feeling that I wasn't going to like living in Munich nearly as much as I liked Kraków or Steyr, but we needed to stay there to wait for our visas so we could leave for America.

It didn't help that my parents decided against enrolling me in school. In spite of my protests, I wasn't able to sway them. "How can you not let me go to school?" I asked them. "How am I supposed to make any friends and have a life?"

"Luncia," Tatu began, "I know this is hard for you to understand, but even though the Nazis have been defeated, there's still a strong anti-Jewish sentiment among some of the people of the city. It's just not safe for you to go to school here."

All of this made me miss Halina terribly. I'd already written her a letter and was anxiously waiting for a reply. But I continued to long for the companionship of someone my age. I'd spend entire mornings gazing out the window of the apartment at the street below, which seemed lifeless in the dull and humid summer air. When I felt like this I had a hard time preventing myself from reminiscing about all the fun I'd had in Austria and what a beautiful country it was in comparison to Germany.

As usual, the only person I had to complain to was my mother. Also, as usual, she managed to listen to my whining without getting too annoyed with me. I think she started to take notice of my changing attitude and feelings about things, because she'd often surprise me in small ways that made me feel like a grown-up. I'd been begging her for some time to let me cut off my long, dark braids, and she always said no. One day in the middle of the afternoon I asked her again. "Give me the scissors," she said with a strange look on her face. She spun me around and I thought she was playing a game with me until I heard and felt the scissors cutting my hair. I couldn't believe it! I was so excited that I started laughing and crying at the same time. I felt so much more mature when I shook out my hair and looked in the mirror.

But although I may have looked more mature, the situation I was in made me feel stuck, and feeling stuck made me feel like a child. I'd try to distract myself by reading for pleasure or going to the movies. I loved the movies—especially musicals—and tried to get my parents to take me as often as I could. There were also Jewish variety shows in the theaters, which were a mix of all different sorts of live musical performances or comedy acts. These were great fun and broke up the monotony of my days.

The only other thing that helped pass the long hours was when neighbors came to visit us in the apartment. A young man named Jack Gruener would come over fairly often. He was a cousin of our landlord and lived in the building, and he spent hours speaking with my father. They'd talk about politics and philosophy and religion. Jack was handsome, clever, and brave—he had survived ten concentration camps as a child. But he never seemed to want to talk with me about anything. I didn't like feeling as if I was being ignored. There were times when he'd walk right past me and not even say hello. At first I took him for an arrogant big shot who thought he was above me, but then it occurred to me that maybe he was just shy and didn't know how to address me.

One afternoon Jack came over to share some poems he'd written and was reading them aloud in the living room. I was curious about what he was saying and so I sat on the edge of my cot pretending to read. Then he got to a part in one of the poems about a goddess of beauty and seemed to be watching me!

"Jack," I said, unable to look him in the eye. "Stop looking at me! You're making me blush!" I was very embarrassed and angry with him.

After that, Jack would speak to me a little more each time he came to visit, which made me think that he had started to respect me and not think of me as a child. I began to look forward to his visits and to talking with him. Within a few months, he was granted his visa and left for America. He promised to keep in touch with us, and so we gave him our family's address in New York.

There was still no word about our visas. We were so eager to leave Germany that we all felt as if the ground we walked on burned our feet. Our relatives in America continued to send us clothes and food, and Tatu started making candy again. With the money they earned from selling it, my parents were able to hire three teachers for me.

My general studies teacher was an elderly woman who was very old-fashioned, and I secretly called her an old maid. She thought that women who wore sheer nylon stockings were indecent! My English teacher was very funny. He only understood English spoken with a British accent, and so that's what he taught me. I learned to use the word *cinema* rather than *movies*, and other expressions that were new to me. For music I went to the teacher's house. Her name was Miss Hierburger. She taught me piano, voice, and an instrument that I immediately fell in love with, the accordion. I enjoyed my lessons with her until one day she confided in me that she was a Nazi sympathizer and said that if another man took Hitler's place, she'd be happy to hide me. When I told my parents what she had said I was never allowed to return to her house again, and for a while I went without a music teacher.

Shortly after this our family received great news. The American consulate notified us that all our documents were in order and had been transferred to the visa department. We were told to immediately schedule our medical exams, blood tests, and inoculations in preparation for leaving Germany.

It was August 1948, and my fourteenth birthday was right around the corner. I couldn't have received a better gift. We had a small party, which was fun, although as always I wished girls my age were there, because all the guests were adults. Genia, who was a good friend of my mother, and her husband, Mr. Winters, came and brought me orange flowers and a manicure set. Tatu bought me a pencil set and my mother got me a blue silk nightgown trimmed with ribbons and embroidery.

I'd had a growth spurt since we'd come to Munich. None of the dresses I had in my closet fit very well anymore, and so my mother decided it was time for me to have a new one. She surprised me again when she came home with a package. Instead of the shorter, more childish style I'd been wearing, she bought me a longer dress with tiny black and white checks and a lovely brown hat that made me look very grown-up.

My parents became concerned that I'd fall behind in piano because I'd completely neglected playing in the months since I stopped studying with Miss Hierburger. Tatu went about finding me a new teacher and decided to contact a Jewish professor whose songs we'd heard on the radio. His name was Mr. Wagner. He came over one afternoon to meet my parents. They liked him so much they hired him on the spot.

I wore my new dress and hat to my first lesson at Mr. Wagner's house. When I arrived, his landlady opened the door and ushered me into his room. Mr. Wagner wasn't there, so I sat down at the piano and lifted the cover and began to play. After about ten minutes, he came in and treated me to a piece of candy before beginning the lesson.

"You're a beautiful young lady, you know," he said to me. "You're going to go very far in the field of music."

He sat down next to me. "And look at your hands," he continued, taking one of my hands in his. "They're perfect for playing." Then he showed me how to correctly position my fingers on the keys. Next, he brought my hand to his lips and kissed it! I was so shocked and embarrassed I didn't know what to do, so I didn't stop him. Suddenly, I grew very cold, probably from nerves, and my hands must have gotten cold, too, because he asked if he could warm both of them in his. I shook my head and pulled my hand away. I wasn't sure if he was being an elegant gentleman or if it was something else. I felt immature and inexperienced.

I didn't know if I should tell anyone what had happened but had a hard time keeping the incident to myself. I decided to confide in Genia rather than my mother because I didn't want to have to stop taking piano lessons again.

"Genia," I began nervously, "something happened at my piano lesson that I'm afraid to tell my mother."

"What?" she asked, sounding slightly alarmed.

"Well . . ." And I let my voice trail off. "Well, Mr. Wagner kissed my hand during my lesson, and I didn't know what to do, so I just pulled it away! I was so embarrassed and wasn't sure if he was just being a gentleman or if it was something more . . ." I trailed off again. "It was absolutely out of line," she said. "Next time you go, don't let him take advantage of you like that!"

"Do you promise not to tell my mother?" I asked.

"I promise for now," she said. "But you must let me know what happens after your next lesson."

For my next lesson, I decided I'd try to defend myself. But just as he had before, Mr. Wagner grabbed my hand to put it to his lips when he was pretending to show me how to place my fingers on the keys. This time I was prepared! I pulled my hand away immediately. He looked embarrassed and began to mumble an apology, and that was the end of my lesson.

The following week I was ill with a cold and missed

my lesson. The week after, my parents asked Mr. Wagner if he would come to our apartment instead of me going to his house because I was still feeling weak. He agreed but then never showed up. And that was the end of my lessons with him!

No one dwelled too much on this because it seemed as if we were closer than ever to leaving Munich. We had our final interview prior to our trip to America and our final medical appointments. I went to the eye doctor and he put drops in my eyes that made it very hard to see for almost five days. We found out that we'd be leaving for America in a week, and then we got a call that we had to leave for the port city of Bremen in two days. We were totally unprepared, of course, but it wouldn't be the first time we had to leave our home in a hurry.

Even though I'd been miserable in Munich, I was sad to leave the city. This may have had more to do with our constant moving from place to place than anything else, and I sometimes wondered if going to America would be worth all the waiting and frustration we'd had to endure. But there was no point in dwelling on the past when we were so close to reaching our goal.

We packed our essentials and planned to leave the majority of our things behind for neighbors, just as we had several times before. But this time my parents decided there was something extra they needed to buy me to take along: a camera. They wanted me to be able to document our journey with photographs, and I was more than happy to do so. "There are so many buttons and knobs," I said to Tatu as I examined the camera. "How will I ever learn to use it properly?"

"Well, we're going to have a long train ride ahead of us," he said. "You'll have plenty of time to read the instructions and practice."

The train ride to Bremen took twenty-two hours, and although the daytime hours were pleasant and I learned how to use my camera, the night was endless. I hardly slept at all. I was exhausted when we arrived at another displaced persons camp, and it was chaos while we were getting settled. Men and women slept in separate quarters, and so my mother and I stayed in a room that had bunk beds. Everyone at the camp was friendly and in high spirits, as they, too, had waited a long time to leave Europe.

We said good-bye to the year 1948 in Bremen. We went to a New Year's party, which was the first real dance I attended, and so beforehand I was very excited. But when I got there, I was disappointed and wanted to leave after two hours. "Somehow I thought it would be different," I told my mother. "I thought it would be more, I don't know, romantic."

"Well," she said, "I can promise you that this won't be your last dance. When we get to America you'll have plenty of dances and parties to go to."

Our ship was the *Marine Flasher*, and it was scheduled to leave on January 7. We'd hoped to sail into New York where our family was, but the best we could do was get ourselves on a boat bound for Boston. We'd have to take a train to New York when we arrived.

All our larger bags had been picked up a day ahead of time, so we only had to carry the smaller bags with us. We left early in the morning for Hamburg to board the ship. The moment I saw the *Marine Flasher* I was completely enchanted and began snapping pictures nonstop with my new camera. "You'd better be more selective about what you take pictures of," Tatu warned me. "Otherwise you'll run out of film!"

"But it's so hard to know," I said. "Everything seems worth a picture! It's all so exciting!"

The ship was immense and wonderful. It had

previously been a military boat, so instead of private rooms we shared common quarters as we had at the camp in Bremen. Mother and I put away our things and arranged to meet Tatu on deck right before we were about to leave.

As the ship began to pull away, there was an uproarious outburst of cheers from everyone around us. People were crying and clapping and waving good-bye to no one in particular. I suddenly felt weightless. My feet didn't feel firmly planted on the wooden deck, and my legs didn't seem to be attached to the rest of my body. I felt as light as air and thought for a moment that I'd begin to float away if Mother's and Tatu's arms weren't around my shoulders, holding me down. As I watched the European shore fade into the distance, I imagined myself to be the heroine of a romantic movie.

Shortly after five o'clock, we were asked to go to dinner. "Mother, look!" I exclaimed when we got to the dining room. "It looks just like the inside of a palace!" There were two beautifully lighted rooms and tables covered in white tablecloths with silver trays of fowl, fruit, and pastries on them. When I entered the dining room I felt more like royalty than like a movie heroine! The ship was so smooth on the water it didn't feel as if we were on a boat, but instead in an elegant restaurant in a fashionable city. Everyone spent hours eating and laughing and enjoying one another's company, and with our stomachs full we went off to bed.

Perhaps eating as much as we did wasn't so smart. At about one-thirty in the morning the boat began to rock so violently that I nearly fell out of bed. People started to feel nauseous and get sick, and seeing people sick around me made me feel sick, too. I held out until about six A.M. but then couldn't any longer, and when I started throwing up, I couldn't stop. The ship's staff told us to go out on deck to get some fresh air, which helped only a little. The next day no one wanted to eat anything except tea, toast, and cookies. Everything everyone had told us before we left Germany about how violent the Atlantic Ocean could be was definitely true.

After three days on the boat we were told to turn back our watches one hour every day for the rest of our journey. This was to help us get used to the time in America, which is some hours behind Europe. Our trip across the Atlantic was supposed to take about ten days, weather permitting, and although we had experienced calm seas for a few days after the initial rockiness, no one expected that we'd continue to be so lucky for the rest of the trip.

Sure enough, after another day or so we hit rough water. Even the crew members were getting sick. We spent most of our time in the lounge, which was in the center of the boat, where we didn't feel the rocking as much. When the waves were especially high, even being in the lounge didn't make a difference. One afternoon it was so bad that I fell off my chair twice and crashed into two other people. That was the same day that I couldn't possibly have eaten if the table in the dining room hadn't been bolted to the floor. Holding on to the table was essential.

We could really only stay in the lounge, in the dining room, and on deck during the day, and at night we had to go to our rooms belowdecks on the ship's sides, where the rocking was worst. There was a woman traveling with an infant and so her room was closer to the deck. One night she invited me to stay in her room with her, so I got a break from the nausea that was keeping me up and was rested the next day and felt much better.

When the ocean wasn't rough, being on board the ship was fun. Looking out at the waves was calming, and I could stare at them for what seemed like hours, watching them climb up and down the sides of the ship. There was a beautiful grand piano on board that I played a few times for a small audience of passengers, as if I were giving a concert. I'd managed to befriend one of the waiters, who seemed to want nothing more than to fatten me up, because he constantly brought me special treats like oranges, apples, and chewing gum. I told him my name had been Luncia in Europe and so he called me Lucille. A kind steward often spent time talking with me, and so my English quickly improved.

Speaking English made me very excited to meet my American family. But as the day we were due to arrive grew closer, I started to worry about what my new life would be like. I had no idea what to expect. Even though I'd been to more than one country in Europe, it was still Europe. Soon I'd be setting foot on completely foreign soil.

Finally, on January 17, 1949, at about eleven A.M., we had our first look at America. There was a lot of noise and excitement on board. People shouted "Hooray!" "Finally, we've made it!" "Thank God it's over! I couldn't have stayed on this boat for one more day!"

We were told to be on deck at one o'clock. Smaller boats filled with newspaper reporters and photographers surrounded the *Marine Flasher*. I went from feeling like a heroine in a romantic movie to feeling like a celebrity waiting to get her photograph taken!

About an hour later we docked and had to stand in line on deck to get our visas. The mayor of Boston made a nice speech, and a military band played the national anthem of the United States, the first time I'd ever heard it. People were so moved by the music that they began to cry. The excitement lasted until about four o'clock, and at last we got off the boat and boarded a train bound for New York.

We arrived at Grand Central Terminal in Manhattan at nearly two in the morning. I was so tired that I felt as if I had started seeing things that weren't there. My mouth was dry and my eyes hurt if I looked up at the bright lights. From the train window I could see children dressed in Polish national costumes waiting to greet us. Volunteers from the American Red

Cross served hot coffee and cookies to people as we got off the train.

We knew that someone from our family would be waiting at the train to meet us, but we didn't know who or what they looked like. As we made our way through the crowd with our luggage, we looked for our names on the signs held up by relatives who'd come to meet family members from Europe. At last we found them. It was our cousin Leon and his wife, who was about twenty years old and quite pretty but turned out not to be very smart.

My parents didn't speak any English and so everyone had to communicate through me. "Hello," I said to them with the best pronunciation I could muster. "It's nice to see you. My parents and I are very happy to be here." It took so much effort for me to say even that. I'd never translated like that before, and it was difficult because I was so tired. After we managed to exchange a few more words I noticed my cousin's wife poke him in the ribs with her elbow. She wanted him to ask me if I wanted some ice cream. He looked at her and shook his head. "Don't you think they make ice cream in Europe? Her parents owned a candy shop in

Poland!" This wouldn't be the first time I'd encounter someone who asked ridiculous questions or made remarks as though we'd come from the Middle Ages.

We got into their car and drove to Queens, where Tatu's sister Rebecca and her husband, Benny, lived. Because it was dark I couldn't see much out the window, but I remember thinking that things looked a lot more modern in America than they did in Europe. "Everything looks so new and shiny," I said to my mother. "It all looks just like the photos that Grandma used to show me." As we pulled up to the house, my aunt and uncle came running out the door to say hello to us even though it was the middle of the night. It was a tearful and bittersweet reunion, and I could tell that my parents were happy to be able to speak with them in Yiddish.

The next morning when I woke up I didn't know where I was. The night before and even the day before that seemed like a dream. When I tried picturing the distance I'd come since leaving Europe, I couldn't wrap my mind around it. The thoughts were too overwhelming.

We had breakfast and Tatu's older brother, Abe, and his wife, Ida, came from Brooklyn to meet us. My parents were overcome with emotion again, just as they had been the night before. Our American relatives had certainly hoped that we'd survive the war, but I don't think they believed we could possibly be standing in that kitchen, alive and well. It was like a miracle for everyone.

Uncle Abe told Tatu that they had found a furnished room for him and my mother but suggested that I live with them. "With David in college now we definitely have the space," Uncle Abe said. "Plus, Ida, being a teacher, can help Luncia with her English."

"It probably would be the best thing for her," my mother said to Tatu.

"I don't want to live without you!" I pleaded. "We were apart for so long."

"But we won't really be apart anymore," Tatu said. "We'll be close by, and we'll see you every day or so. It makes sense for you to stay with your aunt and uncle until your mother and I get settled in an apartment. This way you can start school right away."

Two days later I was enrolled in James Madison High School in Brooklyn with my new, Americanized name: Ruth Gamzer. The night before my first day I was too nervous to eat dinner because I knew my

English wasn't good and I wasn't sure how the rest of the kids would treat me.

Luckily, I was pleasantly surprised. Because I was the only student in the school who had come from Europe, everyone was very kind and treated me royally. My biology teacher liked me a lot and told me to copy homework from one of the other girls in the class to improve my English.

Soon I had a whole entourage of girls waiting to pick me up to go to school and walk me home! I was in heaven, since all my life I'd so desperately longed for the attention and company of girlfriends. A group of girls invited me to join their special social club. I had to participate in their initiation, which meant that I had to wear socks of two different colors to school. I thought it was completely crazy, but I did it because I wanted to belong. All my teachers praised me for Americanizing so quickly.

However, living with my aunt and uncle wasn't so pleasant. Uncle Abe was a chiropractor and so the family had enough money. He treated me to a few new tops and skirts, which I very much appreciated. But Aunt Ida was stingy with food, and I felt as if she took stock of every morsel I put in my mouth.

The worst part, of course, was that I missed being with my parents. My mother had to take two buses to visit, and she'd secretly pack me a sandwich to eat in my room so I wouldn't offend Aunt Ida. She came as often as she could, but it wasn't often enough for me.

One afternoon my mother came with some interesting news. "A letter came to Uncle Benny and Aunt Rebecca's house addressed to Tatu," my mother began. "It's from Jack Gruener! He was living in Detroit, Michigan, with his cousins and then got drafted into the army to fight in Korea, the poor boy."

"That is unfortunate," I said. "He's been through so much, the last thing he probably wanted to do was to go to war."

"You should find some time to write to him," my mother said. "I know you're busy with school and making new friends, but he is a kind person and I'm sure he'd appreciate your letters."

From that day on I tried to write to Jack as often as I could. I'd tell him what living in Brooklyn was like and tried not to complain too much about the situation with my aunt and uncle. After all, he was dealing with a war! I'd only write about the cheery sorts of things that he could look forward to when he came home. At first we exchanged only a letter or so a month, but as time went on our letter writing became more frequent—and more romantic. I sent him a professional photograph my parents had taken of me on my eighteenth birthday, and he sent me the poems he wrote. Even though I went out on dates with a few boys from my class, I always felt that I was saving my heart for Jack.

My father was busy looking for a way to begin working, and before long found a store with a large room in the back where he and my mother could live. Uncle Abe lent my parents money so they could buy all the equipment they needed to start making chocolate and other candy once again.

I couldn't wait any longer to be with my parents, and so I left my aunt and uncle's comfortable three-bedroom house and moved into the store's back room. The table became my bed. Within a month or two we found a lovely three-room apartment right across the street, but I still had to finish out the year at James Madison High School. That first summer vacation I took a job at a doll factory where I painted on lips and eyes. I loved the job because it allowed me to handle the toys I'd craved and been without for so many years of my childhood. In the fall I transferred to Thomas Jefferson High School, which was closer to where we lived. There, I met lots of other European kids, most of whom were also Holocaust survivors. They understood me in a way my American-born friends couldn't.

I graduated from Thomas Jefferson High School in 1952. In my last term I wrote a final assignment for English class, an essay about when I was kept hidden in a trunk for three weeks at the Szczygiels'. My teacher thought it came out so well she recommended it for the yearbook. But a few days later, I got called to the principal's office. I'd never been called in before and was nervous, sure I was in trouble for something—but I didn't know what! The principal sat me down in a chair on the far side of his big mahogany desk. He was smiling, so I knew I couldn't have done anything terribly wrong.

"Ruth," he began, "about the essay you wrote . . ." His voice trailed off.

"Do you like it?" I asked. "I was so happy when it was recommended for the yearbook."

"Well," he began again, "it's an amazingly powerful story you told. You've been through so much—much more than most of the students in this school can even fathom. But that's just the trouble. I don't think the rest of the kids will relate to it. I'm sorry to have to do this, but I can't have the story appear in the yearbook. It's just too sad."

I was shocked by what he said and didn't know how to respond. Finally, after a few moments, I came up with what I wanted to say. "That's a shame," I began, looking him straight in the eye. "Because I don't think it's a sad story at all. If I hadn't survived the war, then maybe. But how can the story of my survival be sad?"

As I walked home from school that day through Prospect Park, enjoying the warmth of the sun on my face, I kept thinking about what I had told the principal. I couldn't always speak my mind in that way—it was something I'd learned over the years. But I believed what I told him more than anything else. I was destined to live, and from that moment on I have always felt it was my duty and privilege to share my story with the world.

Epilogue

After graduating from high school, I continued my education at Brooklyn College and at the New York School of Interior Design.

Jack Gruener and I continued to exchange letters while he served in Korea and I graduated from high school. Shortly after he was discharged, he moved to Brooklyn to live closer to me, and that was when we really fell in love. We had a wonderful courtship and were married on October 4, 1953, not long after I turned nineteen. Jack and I started a successful interior-design firm, and we had two sons, Arthur and Daniel. Arthur is a lawyer and Daniel is a doctor, and they have given us four beautiful grandchildren.

Jack and I live in a house in Mill Basin, Brooklyn, that is decorated with my father's paintings.

Some months later after coming to America my parents opened a little chocolate shop in Brooklyn. The name of the business was Barbara's Chocolates, named after my mother, Barbara. My father, whom my children called Tatu, worked in his shop till his death in 1973. In the later years of his life he began to paint, and this is the artwork that adorns my walls. After my father's death, my mother continued keeping the shop. She hand dipped some chocolates, but primarily she bought candies to re-sell. She passed away in 1989.

And what of those who saved us during the war?

Mr. and Mrs. Oyak never got along. I remember, when we were in hiding, Mr. Oyak telling his wife that he would divorce her after the war and marry a younger woman.

They did divorce, as he predicted they would, and he married a young Jewish girl with whom he had twins. Mr. Oyak's new wife left Poland with the children and went to Israel. She wrote to my parents to ask them to try to influence her husband to join her, as he had promised. Mr. Oyak told my father that he changed his mind about going to Israel, because life in a new country would be too difficult.

Mrs. Szczygiel passed away not long after the war ended. A few years after Mrs. Szczygiel's death, Mr. Szczygiel married none other than Mrs. Oyak! They were very happy together. Mr. Szczygiel and his wife are now both deceased.

In November 2005, I was reunited with the eldest of the Szczygiel daughters, Jasia (now known as Joanna). The Jewish Foundation for the Righteous brought Joanna to New York and arranged our reunion. It was wonderful, and our meeting in the airport was shown on many local news channels in New York City. There was a beautiful dinner in her honor at the Waldorf Astoria Hotel attended by twelve hundred people, including former New York City mayor Rudy Giuliani. Joanna stayed with me and Jack for several weeks and met many of our friends. Joanna is now back in Poland. I speak with her on the phone often.

Today, I give piano lessons, teaching children to share my love of music. I also volunteer as a docent (guide) at the Museum of Jewish Heritage, located in downtown Manhattan, educating children about the Holocaust. Jack and I are also asked to speak at schools, synagogues, and churches all over the country, and tell our story—so that new generations will never forget. We wish for today's children to have a life free of prejudice—so that they and *their* children will not have to suffer as we did.